REENTERING HEAVEN (VOLUME 1 OF 3)

A SEVEN-STEP GUIDE FOR GETTING HOME

WYNE INCE

Edited by
REBECCA INCE
Edited by
MPB0707 (FIVERR.COM)

Reentering Heaven
A Seven Step Guide for Getting Home
© Copyright 2021 by Wyne Ince.
All rights reserved.

This book is an evangelical tool, so you are free to share it.

Contact: wince@reenteringheaven.net

Website: www.bettergetsavedtoday.com

Cover Work: Priscilla Pantin
Last Update: August 28, 2021

Throughout this text, all sections of scriptural references that are bolded, underlined, and italicized were done in this manner by the author for emphasis.

Readers should be aware that Internet websites offered as citations and sources for further information may have changed or disappeared between the time this was written and read. However, the author has made a conscientious effort to choose sites that demonstrate enduring qualities.

PERMISSION STATEMENTS OF VARIOUS BIBLE VERSIONS

- The *New Oxford American Dictionary* and *Oxford Dictionary of English* are the primary sources for all definitional references.
- Scriptures marked KJV are taken from the KING JAMES VERSION (KJV): KING JAMES VERSION, public domain.
- Scripture quotations marked (TLB) are taken from The Living Bible copyright © 1971. Used by permission of Tyndale House Publishers, Carol Stream, Illinois 60188. All rights reserved.
- Scripture quotations taken from the (NASB®) New American Standard Bible®, Copyright © 1960, 1971, 1977, 1995, 2020 by The

Lockman Foundation. Used by permission. All rights reserved. www.lockman.org

- Scriptures marked NKJV are taken from the NEW KING JAMES VERSION (NKJV): Scripture taken from the NEW KING JAMES VERSION®. Copyright© 1982 by Thomas Nelson, Inc. Used by permission. All rights reserved.

❧ Created with Vellum

DEDICATION
FATHER, SON, AND HOLY SPIRIT

I dedicate this book to the only wise, eternal God and Father of Jesus Christ, the Creator of Heaven, Earth, and Hell.

The Lord hath prepared His throne in the heavens, and His kingdom ruleth over all. (Psalms 103:19, KJV)

Can any hide himself in secret places that I shall not see him? saith the Lord. Do not I fill Heaven and Earth? saith the Lord. (Jeremiah 23:24, KJV)

But God demonstrates His own love toward us, in that while we were still sinners, Christ died for us. (Romans 5:8, NKJV)

The Lord openeth the eyes of the blind: the Lord raiseth them that are bowed down: the Lord loveth the righteous. (Psalms 146:8, KJV)

The way of the wicked is an abomination to the Lord, But He loves him who follows righteousness. (Proverbs 15:9, NKJV)

It is impossible to rightly govern the world without God and the Bible.

— GEORGE WASHINGTON

CONTENTS

PREFACE *Why This Book?*	1
HOW TO READ THIS BOOK *Take as Much as You Want*	3
Sections	4
Audiences	5
A STRATEGY AGAINST COVID-19 *My Fight Against It*	6
KEY TERMS AND NAMES *A Quick Look*	17
IT ALL BEGAN IN HEAVEN *The Introduction*	20
REENTERING HEAVEN 101 *Choosing Eternal Life, Not Death*	27
THE BEST AND WORST OF TIMES *The Earthly Experience*	37
GOD AND HIS HUMANS *He Is Not Passive, Only Loving*	44
GOD PROMISES ARE CONDITIONAL *They Are Contractual*	49
THE ENTITLEMENT PROBLEM *Managing Your Claims*	55
THE PURPOSE OF TESTING *An Approach to Creating Value*	62
WHY WE SHOULD PRAY *We Are Not Perfect*	69
LIFE-SAVING QUESTIONS *Answer With the End in Mind*	73
PROMISE WITH UNDERSTANDING *A Potential Trap by Passion*	77
THE REBIRTH OF A FALLEN BEING *Creating a Heaven-Ready Soul*	82
My Experiences and Observations	86

WORK OUT YOUR OWN SALVATION *With Fear and Trembling*	94
Create a Schedule	96
Trust God to Help You	97
ONLY PERFECTION ENTERS HEAVEN *We Must Become Perfect*	99

Section I
60+ THINGS TO CONSIDER
Heaven Is Watching Us

THE JOURNEY'S CHECKLIST *Keep Your Heart With All Diligence*	111
God in All and Through All	111
God Gave Me Today, Not Tomorrow	113
Expectation Management	118
Considering others	123
Forgiveness & Salvation	124
Unexpected Lessons	127

Section II
7 STEPS HOMEWARD
A Guide to Surviving Life on Earth

INTRODUCTION	139
THE SPIRITUAL RACE *Run for Your Life*	146
The Journey's Prayer	151

1. STEP 1 - FORGIVE — 153
   And You Will Be Forgiven
   Week #1

Seek Immediate Forgiveness	155
Avoid Unforgiveness's Penalty	157
Verses About Forgiveness	158
Do This Today and Make It a Lifestyle	159
Summary Points	160

2. **STEP 2 - REPENT**   162
   And Avoid Recurrences
   Week #2

A Cease and Desist Order	163
From Darkness to Light	165
Delaying Repentance	166
A Window of Opportunity	167
Verses About Repentance	169
Do This Today and Make It a Lifestyle	170
Summary Points	171

3. **STEP 3 - PRAY AND FAST**   173
   And Let God's Will Be Done
   Week #3

Efficient Use of Free Will	174
The Power of Words	177
Praying Through the Bible	179
Why We Should Pray	180
A Maintenance Strategy	183
Determination Is Required	187
An Effective Prayer Method	189
Fasting	190
Benefits of Fasting	193
Verses About Praying and Fasting	195
Do This Today and Make It a Lifestyle	196
Summary Points	197

4. **STEP 4 - WORSHIP**   199
   And Draw Closer to Him
   Week #4

The Purpose of Worship	200
Reverence Is Due	201
More Than Drama	203
A Privilege and a Blessing	205
Verses About Worship	208
Do This Today and Make It a Lifestyle	208
Summary Points	210

5. STEP 5 - SERVE — 212
   And You Will Be Served
   Week #5

   - The Nature of a Service — 213
   - Serving God Through Others — 216
   - A Generous Compensation — 222
   - Verses about Service — 223
   - Do This Today and Make It a Lifestyle — 224
   - Summary Points — 225

6. STEP 6 - STUDY — 227
   And Show Yourself Approved
   Week #6

   - Types of Information — 228
   - What the Bible Teaches — 229
   - A Tactical Guide — 231
   - Live the Word by Faith — 234
   - More Than a History Book — 235
   - Nutritional Maintenance — 238
   - Verses About Study — 238
   - Do This Today and Make It a Lifestyle — 238
   - Summary Points — 240

7. STEP 7 - SANCTIFY — 242
   And You Will See God
   Week #7

   - Understanding Sanctification — 243
   - The Impact of Holiness — 244
   - Spiritual Adjustments — 245
   - A Sanctified Soul — 247
   - A Sacrificed Body — 248
   - A Lifestyle of Holiness — 249
   - The Enemy of Holiness — 252
   - Consumption and Behavior — 253
   - Verses About Sanctity (Holiness) — 255
   - Do This Today and Make It a Lifestyle — 255
   - Summary Points — 257

Section III
7 PRAYERS FOR THE JOURNEY
Progressing Through Prayer

PRAYER OF SALVATION *Rescued by Jesus*	263
1. RECOGNIZE YOUR BLESSINGS *Know that God owes us nothing*	266
2. SEEK DELIVERANCE *Cut Ties to Sins*	269
3. STRIVE FOR SOBERNESS *Realize That Evil Intoxicates*	271
4. REMAIN IN CHRIST *Focus on Him: He Is Alive*	273
5. EXERCISE YOUR AUTHORITY *Reign Over Evil*	275
6. PETITION FOR RESTORATION *Live in Harmony With Everyone*	279
7. GIVE THANKS *He Likes to Hear From You*	281
Praise Jesus	283
About the Author	289
NOTES	290

PREFACE
WHY THIS BOOK?

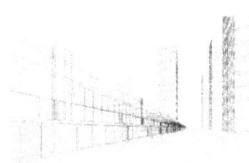

I am simply playing the role of a spiritual and physical actor in this life and the script is not centered on me. There are nearly eight billion more performers on the grand stage called Earth.

This book began in an uneventful way, but it was sheer obedience that oversaw its making. Over the course of about two years, I would awake some mornings overcome by inspiration, and would jump out of bed, rush to my laptop, and record God revelations in a few paragraphs. Then, I whisked it off to an email list of twenty or so people. At that time, I had no inclinations to embark on a book such as this; I had plans for others, to be sure, but not for this one. The writing process only began in earnest once I lost my job after 17 years as a computer professional. In that time of enforced inactivity, I pondered whether to write another iPhone app, continue to write a book, or focus on my next career move. I reached out to God, seeking His guidance for the next step, and He responded through a prophetic buddy whom I greatly respect, Mike.

A clear message emerged: write a book. Though I had a

different writing project percolating at that time, God led me to repurpose the excerpts that I had previously emailed to friends and compile them into parts of the book you are now reading.

Ultimately, this effort is a continuation of a divine instruction I received about eight years ago. On a Saturday morning in early May of 2014, I got out of bed and decided to take a relaxing, leisurely drive in order to reflect on life. But God had other plans for me that day. As I walked into the bathroom, a soft, breeze-like sound whispered into my ear, and I paused. I heard Jesus say, "**Start to write**."

I remained still, expecting to hear more, and then turned slightly toward the voice. But that was all I heard that morning. This inspirational resource that you hold in your hands resulted from that divine prompt. The writing process wasn't initiated because I made a decision to compose this book; rather, this spiritual composition and all of the others came about *because I was supernaturally instructed* and guided to write.

Every day, God whispers His instructions to us through His Holy Spirit. Sadly, few can hear His voice through the hubbub of our hectic, hurried society. Even fewer pay attention, and fewer still act on His instructions.

I am not a theologian, a preacher, or even someone who is academically trained to deliver God's instructions and commands. I am a technologist and a former adjunct lecturer on Computer Information Systems. However, I have been a follower of Jesus Christ for more than 30 years, and during that time, I have gained much wisdom by reading the Bible, and by praising, praying, fasting, and trying to live a respectful life in the presence and sight of God.

Despite how intensely I strive toward a life of holiness, there were moments when I failed quite miserably, hurting both the Comforter and my family. However, my life is significantly better than it used to be. Praise the Lord.

Jesus loves you!

HOW TO READ THIS BOOK
TAKE AS MUCH AS YOU WANT

There are more than 1,200 pages in the Bible.[1] Yet the entire book is principally about one word: love, since God is Love. However, since we are no longer in Heaven or in the Garden of Eden, we are vulnerable to a real enemy. Therefore, the holy writ was expanded, as it were, to include at least two words: love and hate (or, good and evil). As beings fashioned in the image of God, we have to make many, sometimes complicated, decisions. To guide us, God endowed us with

31,000 verses in the form of 66 books, spanning the Old and New Testaments.

Though not comparable to the Bible by any means, this information I present you with will help you steer clear of the many pitfalls set before us by the enemy. This guide is written from the mindset that we are all on a journey, all participants in the race that Paul wrote about in Hebrews 12:1-2.

> *Therefore we also, since we are surrounded by so great a cloud of witnesses, let us lay aside every weight, and the sin which so easily ensnares us, and **let us run with endurance the race that is set before us, looking unto Jesus, the author and finisher of our faith**, who for the joy that was set before Him endured the cross, despising the shame, and has sat down at the right hand of the throne of God. (Hebrews 12:1-2, NKJV)*

Ultimately, this book is just another attempt by God to reach His children—to reach you, if it applies to you. Inside you will find three (3) main sections crafted to ensure that your life has eternal value in the end.

SECTIONS

1. **60+ Things to Consider** - *A checklist of quick and timely soul-saving tips covering a wide variety of topics.*
2. **7 Steps Homeward** - *Simple but mission-critical actions to ensure that we don't run in vain.* Here find strategies to fight the good fight, living productively through forgiveness, repentance, prayer, worship, serving God and others, studying the Bible, and remaining spiritually clean through sanctification. Though order

is not a strict requirement, we can appreciate that forgiveness and repentance go hand in hand. God wants us to seek pardon for our transgressions and don't restart them, as evidence of true repentance.
3. **7 Prayers for the Journey** — *Methods for obtaining divine support as we run for our lives through this dangerous terrain called Earth.*

AUDIENCES

1. If you have **just started the race**, please read sections 1 and 2.
2. If you are **a church leader**, you may consider how you can use section 2 in Sunday school—making it a 7-week course.
3. **Everyone** should use section 3 at least once to say those timely, biblical prayers.

---

1. https://www.reference.com/world-view/many-pages-bible-11cb86032459d8bd

A STRATEGY AGAINST COVID-19
MY FIGHT AGAINST IT

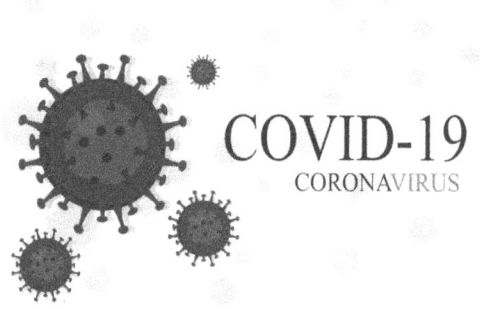

Fear not. Faith is still here.

*H*ello,

I hope you are doing well today, despite the adjustment to a new normal in social interactions around the globe.

In this chapter, I will provide an account of my bout with the symptoms of COVID-19. To that end, I am making this chapter the first one in this guide, although it is one of the very last chapters I wrote. I want to stress the relevance of spirituality in the fight against COVID, not so much to emphasize the threat using statistics but rather to provide some guidance on how to tackle and survive it through Christ— the ever-present Mighty Helper and Healer. COVID has become more than a buzzword. Visit any online or offline business, and you are sure to see a message-based alert reminding you of the present times and conditions of our world.

With this testimony, I desire to explain what has happened to me and how I tackled it. My intention is not different from those who have publicized various home-brewed concoctions of vitamins and the like to fight this pandemic, infamously dubbed COVID. However, I am not nudging you to avoid medical assistance, only reminding you that the Great Physician, Jesus, is always with you and willing to help you, as He helped me that morning from some type of setback, ruin, or worst.

> ***We know that all things work together for the good of those who love God**, who are called according to his purpose. (Romans 8:28, CSB)*

My story of the personal drama began when I awoke one morning in August of 2021, struggling to breathe. The night before, I had started to feel overwhelmingly sluggish, to the point that it seemed as if I were dragging myself around the living room as I casually paced about during a conversation with my wife and daughter. Later that night, I retired upstairs to my workroom, spent upwards of two hours in prayer and praises, and then went to bed feeling my usual self.

However, when I awoke that morning, I found myself struggling to breathe, not in a drowning, panicked manner but still in a way that caused considerable alarm. I began to feel crippled with anxiety as I diagnostically stretched my sore diaphragm to determine if the undue and foreign discomfort was merely a response to some passive physical upset. But no: coupled with my physical uneasiness, a more troubling feeling or presence began to engulf my being. I experienced a menacing, heavy, choking, invisible impact on my inner being, which became my biggest concern. Here I was, lying on the bed combating the attack from two fronts: spiritual and physical. At this time, I began to think about being incapacitated for months (as my neighbor was), about having to call for medical support, and about what would happen to my family should I fall victim to the immediate threat.

Fortunately, my faith in God is strong. I have experienced God's miracle-working grace and mercy in my life while praying for myself and others, and so I feel very comfortable in situations that might be crises for many. The only concern I would have is if God could not help me, if He were sick and couldn't reach me, or if He became deaf or injured. Since none of these is possible, I remain a happy camper. Jesus being alive makes me very happy because I believe my prayer will effectively reach Him when I am in trouble, and trouble is exactly what I experienced that morning.

About that time, I began to pray against the oppressing influence and meditate on what God said to do and not to do. For example, He said, "Don't be afraid, be still," and in obedience, as I have done before in other challenges, I did just that and focused on the fact the He is God and that Satan and sickness are merely tools or opportunities to mature us. I did not want to displease Him by yielding to panic or worry. I knew that electing to condition my soul with a pessimistic mindset would only elevate the situation over His power, which is terrible and should be avoided at all cost. Why? No one can please Him without faith, without relying on His ability to do exceedingly well. After all, He created Heaven, Earth, Hell, and all.

> *Be still, and know that I am God: I will be exalted among the heathen, I will be exalted in the earth. (Psalms 46:10, KJV)*
>
> **Fear thou not; for I am with thee: be not dismayed; for I am thy God: I will strengthen thee; yea, I will help thee;** *yea, I will uphold thee with the right hand of my righteousness. (Isaiah 41:10, KJV)*

A week later, the Lord confirmed my COVID experience when I visited a church some 50 miles away (a long stretch compared to my local worship center just one mile from my home). The invitation came from Mark, someone I had witnessed to (about Christ) roughly four years prior, but had not spoken with for upwards of two years. While driving one day, the Spirit prompted me to call Mark, but of the three Marks on my phone, the one I dialed was not the one I had spoken with most recently of the three. He was a middle-aged man that I had also witnessed to and, by God's grace, prevented from committing suicide. During the Sunday school session, I gave a testimony of my encounter with COVID. Minutes later, the prophetic pastor, Dr. Vanessa Taplah of *The Blessings of God Ministry* at 412 Westside Drive, Lexington, NC, began revealing things about why the Lord allowed me to undergo that period of testing. Of the points she made, this one is perhaps the most important. She explained that what happened to me is similar to God's conversation with Satan about Job in Job 1:8. The pastor declared that Satan is angry because I hold fast to God's word by faith. I rejected the fear that accompanied COVID that morning. Generally, I believe the episode was a sterling example of what faith in God can do for anyone and what God will do for us when we trust in Him.

> *Then the Lord asked Satan, Have you noticed my*

> *servant Job? He is the finest man in all the earth—a good man who fears God and will have nothing to do with evil. (Job 1:8, TLB)*

In the book of Romans, God tells us He will work out all things for the better for those who love Him, which means those who do His will--we love Him through obedience, not just a vocal expression.

Earlier that year, something happened to my financial situation. After being unemployed for about two years, I was expecting to draw some money from my retirement account to hold me over as I looked for another job and considered my next move. However, because of a misinterpretation, or perhaps unclear or incorrect information from a financial advisor, I joyfully reckoned that more funds were available to me than reality would reveal later.

When I reached out to the company to withdraw a certain amount, I found out that only a fraction was available; essentially, I had more than enough to attend to my needs, but I couldn't access it the way I needed it. I was stuck and downright petrified for more than a moment. I did not tell my wife of the financial bind we were in until two weeks later because I needed time to readjust and build up my faith. I felt like a company flush with raw material and equipment but bankrupt from illiquidity, without sufficient cash on hand to run day-to-day operations. I was forced - or called - to live by faith in a new way. I needed money to pay my bills, not to mention my mortgage. However, over those weeks and months, God enabled me to build up faith muscles. In the end, He took care of everything with the infusion of a sizable sum of cash, enough to put me in the clearance for about a year. This evidence of God's mercy prepared me for the COVID events I described above.

> *Consider it a great joy, my brothers and sisters, whenever you experience various trials,* because you know that the testing of your faith produces endurance. And let endurance have its full effect, so that you may be mature and complete, lacking nothing. (James 1:2-4, CSB)

The apparent financial setback was indeed a blessing in disguise, and I never doubted it would be so. Without the unemployment and the subsequent financial advisor-related mix-up, I don't believe I would have had the faith to resist COVID that morning. Perhaps it is for reasons like that that the Bible instructs us to count it all joy when we face trials. God wants us to trust Him. In any case, He was always the provider when I was working. God is here to help us, never the opposite, because He loves us and does not need anything from us.

> *Every good gift and every perfect gift is from above,* and cometh down from the Father of lights, with whom is no variableness, neither shadow of turning. (James 1:17, KJV)

When you face a challenge, don't panic nor fret. Take a deep breath and think about God. Think about His goodness and the fact that He cannot do evil. He is your Father and friend. He is for us. Never doubt that. He is all we have, and we just have to own that truth.

All in all, it is essential to consider that we are first spiritual beings (made in the image of God) and second physical existences (fashioned from dust). Therefore, I believe in the power of the Spirit, God's presence to help, protect, and heal. Ultimately, God alone knows how He would allow each of us to leave this world. Still, I am also aware that fear takes a soul or life to a state of being or condition that displeases God because it is impossible to please Him without faith. Many have fallen victim to fear and have forfeited God's support. I want to help you fight the good fight of faith by encouraging you to trust the only one with the power to save you.

> ***Fight the good fight of faith.*** *Take hold of eternal life to which you were called and about which you have made a good confession in the presence of many witnesses. (1 Timothy 6:12, CSB)*

> ***But let him ask in faith, with no doubting,*** *for he who doubts is like a wave of the sea driven and tossed by the wind. For let not that man suppose that he will receive anything from the Lord; he is a double-minded man, unstable in all his ways. (James 1:6-8, NKJV)*

Faith is the boldness to trust and put confidence in the living, invisible, uncreated, and self-existent God. In other words, faith is to take Him at His word despite the opposing emotional invitations from feelings of worry, anxiety, hopelessness, and restlessness. When you are hard-pressed by the spiritual influence of fright, for example, ask yourself this question: was I born with a twin or extra appendage called fear or distress? Of course, the answer is no. Therefore, such emotions are merely baggage or loads we take on at the courtesy or privilege of our free will. You determine whether to fear or to trust; it's optional and personal.

The story of Job is a remarkable example of long-suffering and determined trust in God, but little is taught about his fear, as mentioned in Job 3:25-26, in which Job noted something that caused him great fear. Essentially, fear is disobedience because

God told us not to entertain it. Faith, on the other hand, is an act of obedience.

> *For the thing I greatly feared has come upon me,* And what I dreaded has happened to me. I am not at ease, nor am I quiet; I have no rest, for trouble comes. (Job 3:25-26, NKJV)

In Hebrews 11:3-11, we see some of the many who benefited from trust in God.

> **By faith we understand that the universe was created by the word of God,** so that what is seen was made from things that are not visible. **By faith Abel offered to God a better sacrifice than Cain did.** By faith he was approved as a righteous man, because God approved his gifts, and even though he is dead, he still speaks through his faith. **By faith Enoch was taken away, and so he did not experience death.** He was not to be found because God took him away. For before he was taken away, he was approved as one who pleased God. Now without faith it is impossible to please God, since the one who draws near to him must believe that he exists and that he rewards those who seek him. **By faith Noah, after he was warned about what was not yet seen and motivated by godly fear, built an ark to deliver his family.** By faith he condemned the world and became an heir of the righteousness that comes by faith. **By faith Abraham, when he was called, obeyed and set out for a place that he was going to receive as an inheritance.** He went out, even though he did not know where he was going. By faith he

> *stayed as a foreigner in the land of promise, living in tents as did Isaac and Jacob, coheirs of the same promise. For he was looking forward to the city that has foundations, whose architect and builder is God.* ***By faith even Sarah herself, when she was unable to have children, received power to conceive offspring****, even though she was past the age, since she considered that the one who had promised was faithful. (Hebrews 11:3-11, CSB)*

— THE EFFECTIVENESS OF FAITH

The apparent challenge to adopt faith might appear harder than deciding whether to eat a cookie or an apple, but that is merely a misperception or misunderstanding of how powerful you are in and through Christ. To appreciably grasp the meaning and obstructiveness of fear (the enemy of faith), think about the uneasiness and dreadfulness that typifies its presence. The capability to fear is not in Heaven, so it is not of God; it is from the underworld, and it is a fine-tuned tactic of the enemy to cripple the soul into listlessness and immobility. Fear shrouds the soul with darkness, thereby creating an atmosphere that counters the light, the very essence of God, Who is greatly displeased when His children, images of Himself, bow to the enemy in cowardice. Our Heavenly Father wants us to perform to the requirement of Hebrews 11:6.

> ***But without faith it is impossible to please Him****: for he that cometh to God must believe that He is, and that He is a rewarder of them that diligently seek Him." (Hebrews 11:6, KJV)*

Help is readily obtainable through Christ, but ignorance of its availability can be detrimental in many ways.

> *My people are destroyed for lack of knowledge: because thou hast rejected knowledge, I will also reject thee, that thou shalt be no priest to me. (Hosea 4:6, KJV)*

God can fix anything, but His skills are not cheap; Satan will not easily resign to allow us to trust in God. The chief enemy of your soul will use the strength and authority permitted by the Lord, though he is merely an agent of evil on a lease—he cannot do as he wishes. He will bombard us with doubt and worry at every opportunity, and we must be willing and prepared to mount steadfast resistance against him. Everything that God allows in our lives is to draw us closer to Him. For instance, an opportunity to exercise extraordinary faith may be the solution to wiping away anxiety from your life. Matthew 19:26 gives us the encouragement that all things are possible with our perfect and merciful Creator.

> *But Jesus beheld them, and said unto them, with men this is impossible; but **with God all things are possible**." (Matthew 19:26, KJV)*

Today, if you believe God created you, then you are implying that you are from Heaven. Since Earth is a transitory place for testing and for demonstrating suitability with Heaven or Hell, where do you think you are heading when COVID is behind you? Yes, you are going back to your Creator. However, what do you think would happen next if the condition of your soul is not suited for living in His eternal presence? I am sure you know the answer. If you are in doubt, it will become more apparent as you read this guide.

> *Now, if any of you lack wisdom, he should ask God— who gives to all generously and ungrudgingly—and*

it will be given to him. ***But let him ask in faith without doubting. For the doubter is like the surging sea, driven and tossed by the wind.*** *That person should not expect to receive anything from the Lord. (James 1:5-7, CSB)*

Thank you.

KEY TERMS AND NAMES
A QUICK LOOK

1. **Devil** (Satan) — Slanderer and accuser. Chief of evil spirits and wicked angels. If God permits, he can afflict human beings with physical and spiritual suffering for their sins, but only to the extent that God allows. For example, in Psalms 103:10-11, we find out that "[God] has not punished us as we deserve for all our sins, for His mercy toward those who fear and honor Him is as great as the height of the heavens above the earth." Being himself sinful, he instigates us to sin and tempts us to do evil. If believers resist his appeals, he will flee from them. Death was brought into the world by sin; thus, the Devil has the power of

death, but Christ has triumphed over him through His death, lovingly and mercifully equipping us to do the same.
2. **God** — The self-existent, uncreated, immortal, invisible Creator and Sustainer of all. Effectively, He has no competition; Satan, for example, is just another of His creations. God does not send anyone to Hell; our decisions do at the courtesy of free will.
3. **Heaven** — The eternal residence of all who refuse Satan's invitation to Hell.
4. **Hell** — The abode of all who reject God's invitation to reenter and rejoin Him in Heaven.
5. **Jesus** — God Himself but in the role of sonship and differs from the Father in one way, according to Matthew 24:36: "Concerning that day and hour [when Christ will return] no one knows, not even the angels of Heaven, nor the Son, but the Father [God] only."
6. **Repentance** — To change one's mind or purpose for the better. In a biblical context, it refers to rejecting sin and turning to God. Christ began His ministry with a call to repentance.
7. **Salvation** — Rescue from sin. It is the spiritual and eternal deliverance granted immediately by God to those who accept His conditions of holiness and faith in the Lord Jesus, in whom alone it is to be obtained (and maintained) upon confession to Him as Lord. In other words, salvation is the blessings bestowed by God on us in Christ through the Holy Spirit.
8. **Satan** (Devil) — Chief adversary, rival, opposer, or competitor. Satan is not simply the essence of evil influences in our heart; he is a real danger to those who seek to reenter Heaven. However, he is doomed and true believers are assured of victory over him.
9. **Sin** — Missing or losing sight of the mark. Rejecting

the will of God and choosing to live according to the lust of the flesh, the lust of the eyes, and the pride of life. Working with Satan instead of with God, siding with evil over good, or opting for Hell instead of Heaven.

10. **Spirit** (soul) — The nonphysical part of a person, also called the soul, mind, or heart, is the seat of one's emotions, character, and decision-making. Similar to the wind or breath, it is invisible, immaterial, and powerful. Spirit (capitalized) refers to the breath of life or Immanuel (God with us, in us).

11. **Soul** (spirit, not Spirit) — The image of God or the immaterial, inanimate, invisible part of a human being. It is the seat of rebirth, personality, appetite, perception, reflection, feeling, desire, and purpose. Both body and soul are the primary constituents of a person. The Spirit (or third member) is our life and represents God Himself in us (Immanuel). The soul is our imperfect or fallen state, while the Spirit is perfection, which is required to create and maintain life.

12. **Test** (trial, examination) — A check for or demonstration of performance, qualities, or the suitability of someone or something. The goal is never to destroy the subject, only to assess and reveal its readiness for an engagement.

13. **Temptation** (lure and snare) — The opposite of testing. Temptation is intended to harm or destroy the subject or target. God only tests us, while Satan and demons tempt us.

IT ALL BEGAN IN HEAVEN
THE INTRODUCTION

See, I have set before thee this day life and good, and death and evil. (Deuteronomy 30:15, KJV)

Even if you have lived the full lifespan of 100 years, it cannot compare to the joy of one day you will experience in Heaven. Heaven is a world where the eternal joy and happiness are continuous.

— A TRIP TO HEAVEN, GEWOOZEE MEDIA

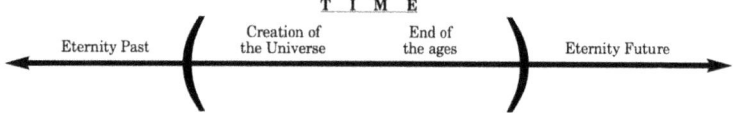

Time is a visible director that the invisible God employed over His creation, mainly to help His children manage resources and events profitably. (Image courtesy of Hope Aglow Ministries, Basic Doctrine Bible Study Course)

*B*efore I even wrote the first sentence of this book, God knew about it. He ordained the day and the time when the writing process would start, when it would end, the opposition I would encounter, and the level of assistance He would have to provide. The Giver and Sustainer of life had a plan; He always does. He foresaw that you would be holding this book in your hand at this exact moment, seeking to connect with Him in some way.

Everything God does has an eternal purpose, never a momentary one. He is not transient; He is infinite. This means that your life and all of its activities are allowed and directed by Him first, and are only subsequently managed by you. His overall plan is designed to ensure that each child gets back home after a lifetime of various tests and temptations at a remote location called Earth. Why does He desire that no one gets off course? He loves us, but He also knows that His human creations like fun times, nice things, and good eats. In order that we may continue to enjoy quality things, Heaven must remain our goal, because the Earth is slated for destruction—and the alternative, Hell, is not merely a figure of speech.

Earth is also a gym, a place where God sends souls to exercise and realize His expectations. The word "exercise" denotes both work and discipline, but do not ever trivialize this word, because failing *this* exercise program does not merely put your weight or your health at risk, but rather puts your *eternity* at risk. The work we perform is not a payment to reenter Heaven; no one could afford that price. Instead, we work to overcome obstacles; we struggle to resist the urge to relapse; and we endeavor to stave off the temptations of joining the enemy's camp, which is often deceptively alluring. The process can be grueling as God transforms the soul into oneness with Himself. As the soul matures into a closer resemblance to Christ, it becomes lighter and brighter with the splendor of God's intimate presence and power, and it readies itself to fly to Heaven when God calls.

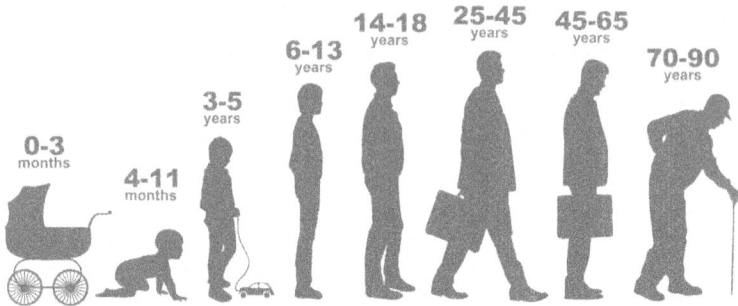

| From cradle to adulthood: the human experience.

From the moment of conception, a human being is the most sophisticated and important life form. The object of God's affection lives in two worlds – the seen and the unseen – owing to its dual physical and spiritual nature. Each life has incredible potential and tremendous responsibility, inherited spiritually from the Father of all. God did not send anyone to Earth to dillydally; we are expected to demonstrate our loyalty and obedience. He plans to reunite with us, and when He does, He will bestow upon us even greater responsibilities, such as ruling over angels. The earthly experience represents a narrow path back to Heaven; it is relatively smooth over some stretches, and almost impassable at other times, swarmed with alluring spiritual danger from every direction. God challenges us with a succession of tests, and even with the equivalent of pop quizzes from time to time to keep us vigilant. God fashioned the journey and pathway, but the desire to travel heavenward is a personal choice, and an eternally rewarding one.

A seed of potentiality germinates every time a baby is conceived. The DNA of that life is the guide, or template, for how that child will physically mature into adulthood and interact with its mortal peers. A baby is more than flesh, blood, and hope; more than a bundle of joy to swaddle. The introduction of a child on this terrestrial orb is akin to the deployment of an ambassador from Heaven, and each child bears a hefty

IT ALL BEGAN IN HEAVEN | 23

responsibility that unique to itself. Even oversight from Heaven is merely support. In His grace and mercy, God will provide sufficient aid for the child to have faith, enabling it to overcome impossibilities. Nevertheless, He will not do everything for the child. Instead, He leaves adequate space for the child to grow, for it to exercise its faith and its patience in preparation for the fight to return to Heaven.

| Responsible to someone or for some action; answerable.

If the totalities of life were mere magic tricks, and we appeared, like Houdini, into a family before disappearing into nothingness, then this guide would prove useless, even ill-considered and pointless. I am sure indulging in other vain, material pursuits would prove tastier and more gratifying. But pursuing that mortal dream is fruitless. Instead, let us wake up to the amazing reality of stewardship and accountability, now that we have matured past the fleeting years of youthful innocence.

When a human being leaves this world at death, it has, indeed, left the mortal world. But the real, **eternally significant** person remains fully awake and alive in a different existence. The phrase "eternally significant" stands in contrast with its inverse: the fleshly member who died as **eternally insignificant** because it could not enter either Heaven or Hell. However, the deceased's soul is eternally significant; the soul is so important that God, through the person of Jesus, suffered unimaginable pain on the cross to allow our soul to enter Heaven.

A human being has three members: body, soul, and spirit. Jesus did not die for the body, which has a relatively short shelf-life and decomposes into molecular tidbits after death. The spirit – the Breath of Life (Emmanuel) – is the embodiment of God Himself living within us, giving us life and spiritual sustenance, and it therefore cannot die. The soul, God's image (likeness, sameness, resemblance, closeness, nature), is the real person, the member that can be welcomed into the dwelling place of the Most-High. When Jesus died for you, He demonstrated that your soul is priceless, more important than the entire world combined. You are so significant that He wishes to preserve you for eternity. But your effort is also mission-critical; preserving your soul cannot be achieved without your faith and involvement.

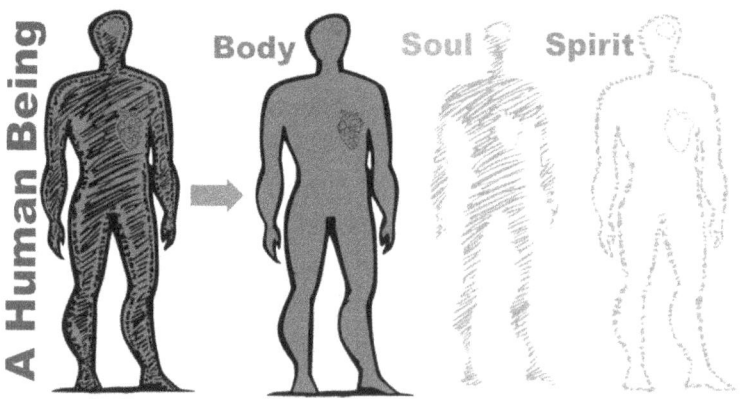

A human being is the composition of body, soul, and Spirit. The body represents the *human* side, while the soul is the *being*. The body dies but never the soul; it's the image of God. The Spirit is God in us; He gives life.

God has created, in His own image, beings (such as you and I) who are expected to serve Him: these are *human beings*. **A** being is a soul which exists in a mortal container. We are souls contained in a *human* container: we are *human beings*, creatures equipped for a purposeful, time-oriented earthly mission.

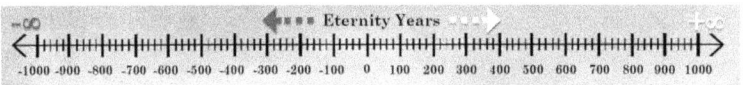

God, the Alpha and Omega, consumes time in His omniscience, in His boundless knowledge of everything. From His ageless viewpoint, time consists of perpetually active events that remain in His memory for as long as the world exists and remains relevant according to His divine discretion. Time exists between the reaches of positive and negative infinity and is accessible by His omnipresence. However, from an earthly perspective, time is a visible, tangible opportunity to choose either Heaven or Hell. Time for us is any marker, any observable point, on a linear number line. Time and free will are marital engagements that are annulled at the Second Coming of Christ. Without the unavoidable requirement to choose good or evil, both time and free will become null and void. More soberingly, time is also the grace or compassion that separates earth and each habitant therein from Heaven and Hell.

Each human being is a child of God, sent from Heaven to Earth for a limited time. Regrettably, far too many children never make it back home to Heaven. We cannot possibly imagine how much this grieves our heavenly Father, especially since He has given us commands in an inspired Book to guide us along our way, to help us make spiritually productive decisions.

God provided the Bible as a Standard Operating Procedure (SOP) guide, and equipped us with prophets, evangelists, pastors, apostles, and teachers; yet many human beings disregard all this instruction and fall instead into eternal ruin. God wants all of His children to fulfill this earthly experience and be ready when He calls them upward. He wants us to understand our purpose in coming here, to embrace the challenges and adversity, to overcome them, and to realize that failing to hear His voice at death translates to eternal separation from Him. Indeed, failing to heed His guidelines and to seek Him wholeheartedly will ultimately lead to eternal confinement in unquenchable fire and terror. Simply put, **God wants His children to comprehend the truth: if they are not serving Him obediently, then they are already slaves of Satan**—and their only hope is to seek repentance.

God never promises eternal life on Earth (as it is today), but only in Heaven. As we prepare to return home, He wants us to learn from the ant, as described in Proverbs:

> *Go to the ant, thou sluggard; consider her ways, and be wise: which having no guide, overseer, or ruler, provideth her meat in the summer, and gathereth her food in the harvest. Proverbs 6:6-8 (KJV)*

Remember, everything we do prepares us to live or die forever. There is no third option.

REENTERING HEAVEN 101
CHOOSING ETERNAL LIFE, NOT DEATH

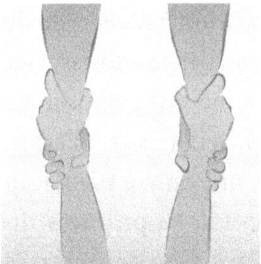

Rescued from sin and its consequences by Jesus Christ.

> *This saying is trustworthy and deserving of full acceptance:* **Christ Jesus came into the world to save sinners**—*and I am the worst of them.* (1 Timothy 1:15, CSB)

On December 2, 2016, a fire in the Ghost Ship nightclub in Oakland, California, left 36 people dead. A few days later, while gazing at a makeshift memorial online and browsing through the sympathy letters and other condolences, I happened upon a sobering parting remark, laced with palpable grief, from one brother to another. The victim had recently graduated with a degree in computer science, and his brother affectionately expressed how brilliant and kind he was. His final words to his beloved brother were, "Love you always." While processing those powerful three words, I began to think about what condition would have to exist for him to be able to express true eternal love for his deceased brother. Both, I reasoned, would have to reenter Heaven, since there is no love in the underworld, wherein lost soul is stripped of everything concerning the nature of God, including love. Jesus came from Heaven and died for everyone so that, for example, these brothers could continue their relationship forever. But this opportunity is not inevitable: we must make the choice to accept His offer of eternal life, or risk losing it forever.

The lifelong connection between the life and death of Christ and our existence in a corporeal vessel called a body or temple is salvation; it is a divine intervention meant to pull us free of the penalty of sin, of being in a fallen state. Being encased in flesh for a lifetime is not only a pivotal mortal experience; it is also a moment, an event, so priceless that I will dedicate this entire chapter to explain. God desires to save everyone.

- **What Can We Offer God?** — One might attempt to respond by listing deed after deed, but the answer is in fact wrapped up in one word: obedience. Why? There are two ingredients or features of compliance with God. From one angle, there is a command from Him to perform a deed, and on the other hand, there is the strength to do as directed. Both the instruction *and* strength come from Him. Our decision is the product of our free will, which is also from God. Therefore, whether a soul obtains eternal life or death depends on its willingness to comply with divine directives. 1 Corinthians 13:3 explains how we love

God. The verse tells that **we love God by doing His will** through obedience to Him. Obedience or rebellion in this sense is a test of stewardship and trustworthiness: free will is a gift from him, and through it He assesses our loyalty and management of this resource. Because obedience is not easy, God compensates it very highly; it pleases Him, because while we have never seen Him, we still step out of the comfort of our visible world and live as He commands through faith.

If I gave everything I have to poor people, and if I were burned alive for preaching the Gospel but didn't love others, it would be of no value whatever. (1 Corinthians 13:3, TLB)

The one who obeys Me is the one who loves Me; *and because he loves Me, My Father will love him; and I will too, and I will reveal Myself to Him. (John 14:21, TLB)*

But without faith it is impossible to please Him, for he who comes to God must believe that He is, and that He is a rewarder of those who diligently seek Him. (Hebrews 11:6, NKJV)

If you are willing and obedient, you will eat the good things of the land. *But if you refuse and rebel, you will be devoured by the sword." For the mouth of the LORD has spoken. (Isaiah 1:19-20, CSB)*

- **How Many Times Should We Forgive?** — The command to forgive others is a divine order to the soul, which is the image of God. The soul decides whether to obey or disobey using the power of free will. Pardoning someone once might be achieved with effortless patience and compassion; however, when the requests for forgiveness become more common, the soul may build a wall of resistance fortified by frustration and anger. The person may then cry out, "Lord, how many times must I forgive this offender?" His response would be to study Matthew 18:21-22. Note that I did not use the word "read," but rather "study." Why? Merely *reading* the verse might prompt you to eagerly enter 70x7 in your calculator, but the result of 490 has a deeper meaning, which Psalms 90:10 partly provides. I believe 70x7 means to forgive someone seven days a week for the estimated lifespan of 70 years—essentially for a lifetime. Moreover, 490 cannot be the answer because what would happen if the person offends you for the 491st or 492nd time? Matthew 6:14-15 places a condition on our guarantee of receiving forgiveness from God—we must first forgive others. Perhaps a deeper appreciation for 70x7 is reflected in our imperfection: there is no limit to the number of wrongs a person can commit as a fallen, eternal being of limitless potential. Therefore, 490 could just as easily be perceived as the symbolical directive to forgive an infinite number of times.

> *Then Peter came to Him and said, Lord, how often shall my brother sin against me, and I forgive him? Up to seven times?" Jesus said to him, I do not say to you, up to seven times, but up to **seventy times seven** [70x7]. (Matthew 18:21-22, NKJV)*

> *The days of our lives are **seventy years**; and if by reason of strength they are eighty years, Yet their*

> *boast is only labor and sorrow; For it is soon cut off, and we fly away. (Psalms 90:10, NKJV)*

> *For if you forgive men their trespasses, your heavenly Father will also forgive you. But **if you do not forgive men their trespasses, neither will your Father forgive your trespasses**. (Matthew 6:14-15, NKJV)*

> *For **rebellion is as bad as the sin of witchcraft, and stubbornness is as bad as worshiping idols**. And now because you have rejected the word of Jehovah, he has rejected you from being king. (1 Samuel 15:23, TLB)*

- **When Does a Person Die?** — This is not a trick question. Most people associate death with finality, burial, or cremation. That perspective is only partially correct because it presupposes that a person is constructed only of the flesh. However, since we are body and soul, we have two lives and two deaths: the passing away of the body and of the soul. Jesus came and died for the soul. Why? The soul is the decision-maker made in God's image and is capable of obedience and disobedience, choosing or rejecting Him under the auspices and privileges of free will. Which did God create first? The body or soul? Genesis 1:26 reveals that God's image, or our soul, was first created. So how do we know our soul is His image? 1 Timothy 1:17 says God is invisible, as our souls are. Our physical bodies came onto the stage of life and time in Genesis 2:7 when God formed us from dust. So again, we approach the question: when does a person die? Does the answer depend on whether we refer to the body or the soul? By the way, the Spirit cannot die—God is the Spirit, the life in us. The great answer to the question is that the soul dies a spiritual death first that separates it from God and from Heaven. Spiritual death is the result of living an unrepentant life. Until repentance, that person is already in Hell and will materialize there on final breath. The reason the spiritual death is the first member is divine and logical: before a person dies, all decisions must be made because mercy and grace do not apply to a soul after physical death.

> *Then God said,* ***Let Us make man in Our image****, according to Our likeness; let them have dominion over the fish of the sea, over the birds of the air, and over the cattle, over all the earth and over every creeping thing that creeps on the earth. (Genesis 1:26, NKJV)*

> *Now to the King eternal, immortal, invisible, to God who alone is wise, be honor and glory forever and ever. Amen. (1 Timothy 1:17, NKJV)*

> *And the LORD God formed man of the dust of the ground, and breathed into his nostrils the breath of life; and man became a living being. (Genesis 2:7, NKJV)*

- **Who Does the Earth Revolve Around?** — This question is perhaps the most crucial and far-reaching one because it calls us to focus on a very subtle truth. Science teaches us that the Earth takes 365 days to revolve around the sun, but have you ever considered that each life, each person, also completes a rotation in its lifetime: a rotation around the Son, the only begotten Son of God. Regardless of race, color, nationality, or religion, everything we do is done for Him and through Him because we use energy, which is life, and He is the giver and sustainer of life. One might argue that sinning is for the devil, and I will tell you the Earth is the Lord's and the fullness thereof (Psalms 24:1). Satan owns nothing. Sin, however, is mismanagement of God's life and His time in us; in other words, while sin is indeed a production of the soul, it is not to God's quality, and so He rejects it. We are held accountable for wasting His resources, for being unprofitable, for producing something that cannot enter Heaven.

- God lives in us, so you and I are His temples. God has over 7 billion temples across seven continents; each of these places or bodies of flesh, from which God demands holiness, yearns and strives to meet life's essentials through activities of the soul, the decision engine that processes desires. It is perhaps evident at this point that God created the soul to work in harmony with Him and to worship Him, but we cultivate disharmony through disobedience or resistance. Still, the soul requires Him for the spiritual energy needed to function, and, similarly to the soul, the body also operates through the fuel He gives through each breath. There is more to this point. Think about these truths for a moment: 1) A person's Spirit is God's life and presence in a body; 2) God created the soul to worship Him; 3) The divinely planned union of soul and Spirit resides for a lifetime in a house or container; and 4) Every day, throughout the world, we perform a duty of maintaining God's temple through an enjoyable process called eating or feasting.

- Eating is a lifelong reparative campaign God has assigned to each person to maintain His temple, a body made of dust. Since His yoke is easy and His burden light compared to what the enemy imposes upon a soul, He gives us upwards of 10,000 taste buds to enjoy the maintenance process.

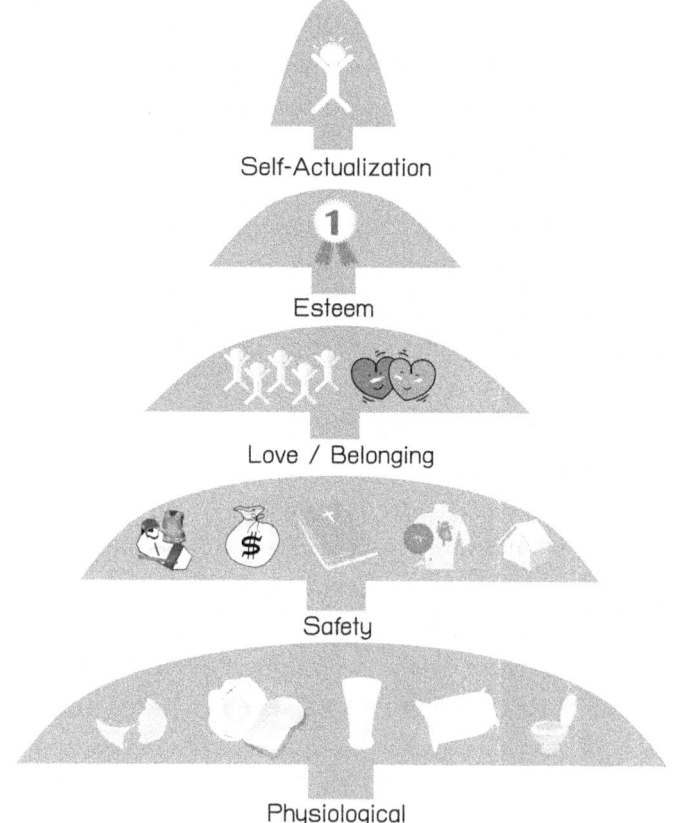

Maslow's Hierarchy of Needs

> *And the LORD God formed man of the dust of the ground, and breathed into his nostrils the breath of life; and man became a living being. (Genesis 2:7, NKJV)*

> *Come to Me, all you who labor and are heavy laden, and I will give you rest. Take My yoke upon you and learn from Me, for I am gentle and lowly in heart, and you will find rest for your souls. For My yoke is easy and My burden is light. (Matthew 11:28-30, NKJV)*

- Therefore, whether a person believes in God or not, they are fundamentally involved in supporting His missions on Earth. No one can escape working for or interacting with God. The only undetermined thing is whether one's connection will have been profitable or not; was it suitable for Heaven or Hell?
- Maslow's Hierarchy of Needs is a comprehensive categorization of our five basic needs: physiological needs, safety, love, esteem, and self-actualization. According to Maslow's reasoning, if we were not living in this physical or natural realm, his model's foundation of physiological and safety needs would prove useless. However, we *are* on Earth, and maintaining ourselves consumes us ceaselessly. A person may endure a socially impoverished life, but a hungry, starving body soon succumbs to energy depletion. There is an American proverb that says, *"The squeaky wheel gets the grease."* In this instance, the wheel is unfortunately the body, not the soul. In the end, the body will pass away, but the soul will not. The body is visible, so we readily present it to the world and our prideful hearts are unwaveringly

concerned with maintaining it, if only for pomp and circumstance. We too often neglect the only thing we truly have and what is most important to God: our soul, the image of God. Jesus suffered and died to get our souls back to Heaven, to redeem them in the image of Himself. Therefore, as the Earth silently orbits around the sun year after year, consider that you and I also perform an inescapable rotation called a lifetime. Strive to ensure that the moving parts in your rotation, all your decisions and your actions, are in sync with the divine system in Heaven, else it will be discarded for misalignment.

Our souls are valued by and anchored on obedience and prompt forgiveness of self and others. The term "dead person walking" describes a soul living in disobedience who would end up in Hell if not rescued with timely repentance.

THE BEST AND WORST OF TIMES
THE EARTHLY EXPERIENCE

| Life and time

> *To everything there is a season, a time for every purpose under Heaven. (Ecclesiastes 3:1, NKJV)*

Charles Dickens, author of A Tale of Two Cities, was not only a talented novelist, but also a soul of spiritual depth that God presented to the world on February 07, 1812, in Portsmouth, England. An example of his literary wit and contemplative persona is evident in the thought-provoking and intriguing excerpt below.

> *It was the best of times, it was the worst of times, it was the age of wisdom, it was the age of foolishness, it was the epoch [or notable period] of belief, it was the epoch of incredulity [or unwillingness or inability to believe], it was the season of light, it was the season of darkness, it was the spring of hope, it was the winter of despair.*
>
> — CHARLES DICKENS, A TALE OF TWO CITIES

> *A time to be born, And a time to die; A time to plant, And a time to pluck what is planted.*
> *A time to love, And a time to hate; A time of war, And a time of peace.*
> *A time to weep, And a time to laugh; A time to mourn, And a time to dance.*
> *A time to gain, And a time to lose; A time to keep, And a time to throw away.*
> *A time to kill, And a time to heal; A time to break down, And a time to build up.*
>
> — ECCLESIASTES 3, NKJV)

Research indicates that the famous quotation—"the best of times and worst of times" —describes contradictions, emotions of suppression, and the hope felt by the citizenry of London and Paris (the two cities) leading up to and during the 18th century French Revolution. Even though a peek into Dickens's biographical history does not unveil anything ostensibly religious, his campaign letters for children's rights, education, and other social reforms provides more than a hint of his spirituality and care for other mere mortals.

I admire how Dickens artistically and poetically portrays the dualities and conflicting sentiments that engulfed his European compatriots. Since we are made in the image of God, we share many of His characteristics, and a story of this striking similarity is found in Isaiah 45:7, where we are introduced to two sides of God, love and justice (or judgment). This verse is so important that I have provided four translations below.

> *CSB Translation: I form **light and create darkness**, I make **success and create disaster**; I am the LORD, who does all these things.*
>
> *TLB Translation: I form the **light and make the dark**. I send **good times and bad**. I, Jehovah, am he who does these things.*
>
> *NASB Translation: The One forming **light and creating darkness**, causing **well-being and creating disaster**; I am the LORD who does all these things.*
>
> *NKJV Translation: I form the **light and create darkness**, I make **peace and create calamity**; I, the LORD, do all these things.*

The verse, in one way, encourages careful rumination on how God uses different seasons and occasions to prompt us to look heavenward and acknowledge our dependence on Him. Yet, in another light, the passage of Scripture deliberately awakes us from the ill-conceived notion that God does not allow or ordain hardship to mature us to be more and more like Jesus.

Today, in the year 2021, without appealing to or inviting pessimism, we are indeed living in troubling and tumultuous times of startling dualities: a time of relative peace in some regions and raging wars in others; a period of proliferating online churches and dwindling congregants in brick-and-mortar churches; a devastating pandemic and localized effort to fight them. Still, and from an overarching view, and at least from *my* view, Earth is the best and worst of places to be. I will explain.

God created us; He remains in Heaven, but we are on Earth. He is entirely spiritual and invisible, while we are both spiritual and visible. We are encased in mortality; He is not. He cannot change from His perfection in holiness; we cannot change from our imperfection without Him. We often waffle about whether to return to Heaven or to continue the natural orientation of a fallen being such as us. Living in this infinitely remote location is considerably discomforting because we are not from here; we are aliens in this land. From this perspective, **Earth is the worst place and time** because we must fight to get back home in a condition that is acceptable to Him, without stains or wrinkles, as a soul suitable for Heaven. If we mess up by leaving this world or dying without a relationship with God, then only the fate of fallen angels awaits: the Lake of Fire.

> *But now He has reconciled you by His physical body through His death, to present you holy,* ***faultless,*** *and* ***blameless before Him.*** *(Colossians 1:22, HCSB)*

There is another perspective, one where **Earth is the best of places and times**. This perspective simply requires we compare Earth to not Heaven, but rather Hell. Why? To appreciate this explanation, we must embrace the truth that, like the fallen angels who were booted off of the Celestial realm, we are also fallen beings, we were also created by God. However, for reasons known only to God, Lucifer and the angels who sided with him in The Rebellion were eternally separated from God that instance. We who are also fallen are given a redemptive opportunity on the Earth, but it is a probation period, a last chance to reconcile with God through Jesus. The blessedness of this planet is perhaps most appreciated by lost souls. Everyone who did not return to the heavenly kingdom is plagued by deep anguish and eternal regrets.

> *Stop loving this evil world and all that it offers you, for when you love these things you show that you do not really love God; for all these worldly things, these evil desires—the craze for sex, the ambition to buy everything that appeals to you, and the pride that comes from wealth and importance—these are not from God. They are from this evil world itself. And this world is fading away, and these evil, forbidden things will go with it, but whoever keeps doing the will of God will live forever. (1 John 2:15-17, TLB)*

Another familiar duality of the best of times and the worst of times is what I would call the tale of two dreams: a blissful dream and a terrifying dream. Dreams ordinarily fall into one of two types: those you wish would never end and those you wish had never started.

Some time ago, while I was praying, I believe the Lord gave me a powerful insight into the nature of a dream, especially for someone who did not make it back to Heaven. Have you ever considered why a person who has fallen asleep might later spring out of a horrific nightmare, with sweat coating their body and their heart beating fast? Sweat is typically associated with work, the movement of body parts. In a bad dream, then, the body may respond as if you had been on a treadmill for some time.

Medically, the term used to describe this dream-and-body or soul-and-body interplay is "psychosomatic response", a condition in which mental or soul-based factors cause physical responses (though, of course, a doctor won't use the word "soul" but will opt for the more psychologically-friendly "mental"). The soul is like a massive engine; the body is no match for it because the soul is infinite while the body is finite. The soul and body are so tightly interwoven, though, that certain outputs of the soul are distributed in the body. For example, what is stress or fear? These are the actions of the soul that are transferred to the body.

During a nightmare, someone or something may attack you with a weapon, yet you will emerge from that terror without a scratch. Why? You are still alive; only your soul was engaged in that horrific scenario. However, if God did not allow you to wake up and you were not prepared for Heaven, you will be lost to all contacts, forever entombed by your sins in that dream-like state. Matters get still more complicated and eternally impactful. While the body on Earth would no longer function, you would get a new body, an immortal one that will never die. It is with this new eternal body you will feel the pains and tortures associated with Hell. In other words, a person who dies in Christ enters the bliss of Heaven, while the unsaved are lost, eternally separated from God, and must face the full penalty of sins without grace or mercy. I am sure no one wants to die in that terrible dream-like yet vividly real spiritual state. Earth is the best of places and times only for those who depart from it spiritually alive.

> *A wise man's heart discerns both time and judgment,*
> *because for every matter there is a time and*

judgment, though the misery of man increases greatly. (Ecclesiastes 8:5-6, NKJV)

Because the sentence against an evil work is not executed speedily, therefore the heart of the sons of men is fully set in them to do evil. (Ecclesiastes 8:11, NKJV)

GOD AND HIS HUMANS
HE IS NOT PASSIVE, ONLY LOVING

So God created man in His own image; in the image of God He created him; male and female He created them. (Genesis 1:27, NKJV)

God created us, but today we are miles from home, on Earth today; not that one can commute to the celestial shore using traditional methods, anyway. He alone knows why you and I are not in Heaven at this time, and He alone knows the path each one must take to return to Him.

Humans are ordinarily internally complacent, motivated by

external threats and trinkets; we usually need something beyond ourselves to get us going, since necessity is the mother of invention. A threat to our comfort causes us to mount a defense, while a gift makes us relaxed and welcoming. With that mindset, many recognized God as the Trinket, as everything that is tasty and not medicinal. Some misread his calm and sweet nature as passivity, but His love belies – only for a grace period – the threat that His anger can wield against sin.

Earth is not an excursion or a picnic. You may say, "Sure, I know that." However, if your life does not reflect what you say you are so sure about, them whom are you trying to fool? Everyone is seeking comfort, pleasure, rest, and relaxation, but that is a tall request and an unreasonable expectation for fallen beings now facing a final chance to avoid permanent separation from Heaven and eternal ruin.

Many don't understand the blessed opportunity and grave spiritual condition that they have entered into as earthlings. A more disturbing perspective comes into focus when we consider that years spent in stubborn isolation from God have imbued countless young and old with beliefs and doctrine that only widen the link to spiritual civilization. You may see this as an opposing point of view, but keep in mind that my goal is to offer help, and that I might be a tad bit more informed on this subject matter owing to research, spiritual impartation, or both.

I am firmly aware that God is the active overseer or ruler over all; nothing gets by Him. While free will enables us to either accept or reject Him, Hobson's choice translates into an idiom – "take it or leave it" – that adequately describes the only type of relationship God expects from us: we accept and serve Him totally or not at all. Similarly, adhesion is a word used in the insurance industry to stipulate that the contract terms are fixed. When you enter a contract, you accept it as-is; in other words, you take it or leave it. This is to say that we cannot serve God and someone or something else at the same time.

It is crucial to understand and thoroughly appreciate that God does no wrong, despite the plentiful examples of evil in the world. Yes, He allows many things to happen. Otherwise, where and would how would free will operate? Moreover, a person might change when a threat is present or looming. Who can subject God to compromise? He cannot perform evil because He would become dark, imperfect, and fallen; He would no longer be God, and we would not exist because His perfection and love hold everything in its place.

It is easy to reason that someone can love God more than anyone else, even though we cannot see Him. But is this even possible? The answer is no, it is not. 1 John 4:20 says," If anyone says, 'I love God,' and yet hates his brother or sister, he is a liar. For the person who does not love his brother or sister whom he has seen cannot love God whom he has not seen." On this account, we understand that we must love God through others. Love is an action word that is fueled by a pure heart. We nurture good thoughts about others, and, as God would do, we demonstrate kindness. Love is flawless because God is love. When we respond with unkindness, bitterness, selfishness, and the like, it shows that we need more of God's presence in us. The darkness associated with those ill feelings must be purged to allow the nature of God to live in and through us.

God does not have favorites. To imply that He loves one person over another would suggest that He is a liar and an imperfect deity. God cannot change, so His love cannot vary. As the totality of love, He cannot give a portion of Himself else love will be broken. Moreover, since we are all His images, what kind of parent would He be to demote or promote His love toward any of us? Still, do not be carried away by His love for you. Justice and judgment are the two Js to ascribe to Him, because He does not tolerate sin from anyone. Justice will punish the bearer of unrepented sin. His justice system is a body of spiritual and natural laws – a divine constitution – that applies the rules of sowing and reaping to everything planted, whether good or evil.

> **For great is the LORD, and greatly to be praised; he is to be feared above all gods.** For all the gods of the peoples are worthless idols, but the LORD made the heavens. (Psalms 96:4-5, ESV)

> **O worship the LORD in the beauty of holiness** [this is how we truly worship and honor Him]: fear before him, all the earth. (Psalms 96:9, KJV)

> **You who love the LORD, hate evil!** [do you like gossip, backbiting, vengeance, fornication, etc.?] He protects the lives of his faithful ones; he rescues them from the power of the wicked. (Psalms 97:10, CSB)

> **Serve the LORD with gladness;** come before him with joyful songs. Acknowledge that the LORD is God. **He made us, and we are his—his people, the sheep of his pasture.** (Psalms 100:2-3, CSB)

> **Enter into his gates with thanksgiving,** and into his courts with praise: be thankful unto him, and bless his name. (Psalms 100:4, KJV)

> **The LORD is compassionate and gracious, slow to anger and abounding in mercy.** He will not always contend with us, Nor will He keep His anger forever. **He has not dealt with us as our sins deserve** or repaid us according to our iniquities. For as high as the heavens are above the earth, so great is His faithful love toward those who fear him [to

fear Him is to do His will, to abstain from sin].
(Psalms 103:8-11, NASB)

As a father pities his children, So the LORD pities those who fear Him. For He knows our frame; He remembers that we are dust. (Psalms 103:13-14, NKJV)

But the mercy of the LORD is from everlasting to everlasting upon them that fear him, and his righteousness unto children's children. (Psalms 103:17, KJV)

GOD PROMISES ARE CONDITIONAL
THEY ARE CONTRACTUAL

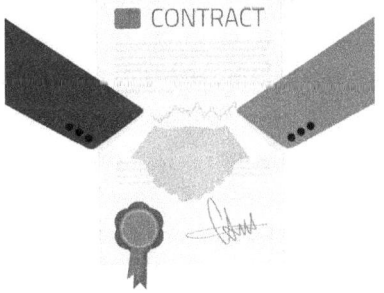

> **A Condition: 1)** Whatever you do, do it enthusiastically, as something done for the Lord and not for men, **2)** knowing that you will receive the reward of an inheritance from the Lord. (Colossians 3:23-24, HCSB)

A constitution is a body of fundamental principles according to which a state or other organization is governed. A legal or social code, written or not, bears a similar authority, directing how people should interact with each other and the consequences of misbehavior. Laws are meant to identify, correct, or even punish breaches in the code. Every action can arguably be considered a binding contract, since it evokes a reaction, whether immediately or delayed, seen or unseen, realized or unrealized. When we work for someone, we expect to get paid an amount based on our perceived value or worth; your wages, then, is conditional. Both Matthew 5:12 and 2 Corinthians 5:10 provide examples of a comparative reward or compensation system in Heaven and Hell: what we do on Earth corresponds to and mirrors how we will be rewarded in the hereafter.

> *Rejoice and be glad,* ***for your reward in Heaven is***
> ***great****; for in this same way they persecuted the*
> *prophets who were before you. (Matthew 5:12,*
> *NASB)*

> *For* ***we must all appear before the judgment seat of***
> ***Christ, so that each one may receive***
> ***compensation for his deeds*** *done through the body,*
> *in accordance with what he has done, whether good*
> *or bad. (2 Corinthians 5:10, NASB)*

Nothing is one-sided; there are counterbalances and consequences for everything that this life and time produces. Even the response to the salvation prayer is conditional, because God sees whether one's heart is serious or not. When God created the world, it became a living, non-discriminatory natural and spiritual enterprise, capable of responding precisely and consistently to every request for interaction from humans, for example.

God, through Jesus, created and oversees through His omnipresence and omniscience the application of all spiritual and natural laws. We see reference to this truth in Isaiah 9:6: "For a Child will be born to us, a Son [Jesus] will be given to us; and the government will rest on His shoulders." Jesus' authority is the Government of governments, as He is also the King of kings and Lord of Lords. Colossians 1:16 reveals the construction process: "For by Him [Jesus] all things were created, both in the Heavens and on Earth, visible and invisible, whether thrones, or dominions, or rulers, or authorities—all things have been created through Him and for Him." Because of His holiness and unchangeability in comparison with our imperfection and wavering nature, contractual conditions must be in place if we want to measure up to Him. These conditions are repentance and petition, both of which are one side of the divine contract for gaining support from Heaven. God is willing to help us, but if we don't actively pursue our own side of the agreement by abstaining from sinful ways and making prayerful appeals to Him for help, we will not benefit from the supernatural system that governs the world, as we see in Matthew 7:7-8 and Psalms 7:11-12. Certainly, God loves us, but He does not wink at sin nor tolerate it from anyone.

> *Ask, and it will be given to you; seek, and you will find; knock, and it will be opened to you.* For *everyone who asks receives, and the one who seeks finds, and to the one who knocks it will be opened.* (Matthew 7:7-8, ESV)

> God is a just judge, and **God is angry with the wicked every day** [because they are destroying themselves]. If he does not turn back, He will sharpen His sword; He bends His bow and makes it ready. (Psalms 7:11-12, NKJV)

> **How precious also are Your thoughts to me**, O God! How great is the sum of them! (Psalms 139:17, NKJV)

It is careless and ill-advised to perceive God as a source of unconditional support or help; if he were, where would the notion of sowing and reaping apply? We read in Matthew 5:45 that He allows the rain to shine on the just *and* the unjust, but it is perhaps not for the reason many might think. God wants to apply grace and mercy and to lessen distractions in our lives, particularly when we commit a transgression. Can you imagine the chaos of interference, obsession, and immediate judgment that would occur if He were to turn on and off sunshine and rain person by person, household by household? No; it is both convenient for and merciful of Him to provide our basic needs so that we can focus on the bigger personal and private concerns in preparation to crawl, stride, and sprint along the narrow path of forgiveness and repentance toward Heaven. After all, we are only children in His sight.

Therefore, the 'Name It and Claim It' exhortation from some pulpits is advisable, even truthful when the prerequisites are first addressed. We must do as God directs before embarking on a 'Name It and Claim It' campaign. For instance, if you doubt the preconditions of your petition, study the Bible or reach out to someone who can offer sound guidance. Yes, there are foundational requests that God will answer right away, such as a prayer for forgiveness and repentance. Prayers of that kind are the cornerstone of a relationship with Him and must be in place to support the connection between you and Him. However, other prayers may not be as promptly granted. A prayer for financial blessing, for instance, from someone not in right-standing with God might be ignored until the petitioner repents and turn back to Him. God might even opt to deny the request because it may cause more damage than good. Our hearts must be ready to receive showers of blessings, else we may drown in pride or greed. God wants the best for us, but whether we receive it is conditional upon our choices.

Following are some verses that emphasize the conditional

element of God's promises. Please also read Deuteronomy 28 for a comprehensive insight of blessings for obedience and curses for disobedience.

> *If any of you lacks wisdom, let him ask God, who **gives generously** to all without reproach, and it will be given him. **But let him ask in faith**, with no doubting, for the one who doubts is like a wave of the sea that is driven and tossed by the wind. For that person must not suppose that he will receive anything from the Lord; he is a double-minded man, unstable in all his ways."* (James 1:5-8, ESV)

— CONDITION: FAITH, NOT DOUBT

> *Truly I say to you, whoever says to this mountain, 'Be taken up and thrown into the sea,' and **does not doubt in his heart, but believes that what he says is going to happen, it will be granted to him.** "Therefore, I say to you, all things for which you pray and ask, believe that you have received them, and they will be granted to you.* (Mark 11:23-24, NASB)

— CONDITION: FAITH, NOT DOUBT

> *Ask, and it will be given to you; seek, and you will find; knock, and it will be opened to you. For everyone who asks receives, and the one who seeks finds, and to the one who knocks it will be opened."* (Matthew 7:7-8, ESV)

— CONDITION: PRAYERFUL PERSISTENCE

> *Truly, truly, I say to you, whoever believes in Me will also do the works that I do; and greater works than these will he do, because I am going to the Father. Whatever you ask in my name, this I will do, that the Father may be glorified in the Son. If you ask me anything in my name, I will do it.* (John 14:12-14, ESV)
>
> — CONDITION: BELIEF

> *And **whenever you stand praying, forgive**, if you have anything against anyone, so that your Father also who is in heaven may forgive you your trespasses.* (Mark 11:25, ESV)
>
> — CONDITION: FORGIVENESS

> *Therefore I tell you, **whatever you ask in prayer, believe that you have received it, and it will be yours**.* (Mark 11:24, ESV)
>
> — CONDITION: BELIEF

> *Because **he is lovingly devoted to Me [he obeys Me]**, I will deliver him; I will protect him because he knows My name.* (Psalms 91:14, HCSB)
>
> — CONDITION: OBEDIENCE

THE ENTITLEMENT PROBLEM
MANAGING YOUR CLAIMS

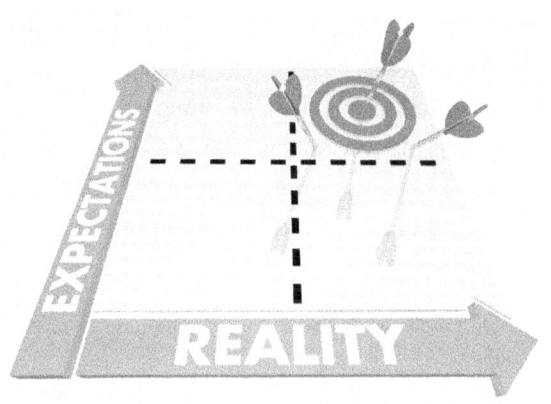

I lift my eyes toward the mountains. Where will my help come from? ***My help comes from the LORD, the Maker of Heaven and Earth.*** *(Psalms 121:1-2, CSB)*

Someone's accountability to God and others should be objective, not subjective. Conflicts of interest and social collisions occur when we seek to highjack someone's life with subjectivity, with what *we* deem fitting for them. Not even

God attempts that. Through the lens of objectivity, we accept people for who they are and pray for God to help them make eternally beneficial life choices. Each person, each soul, is entitled by its Creator to its own management of life and time.

Our souls, having been fashioned in the image of God, maintain a connection with Him and can spontaneously cry out to Him when overwhelmed, because we feel entitled to our Creator's assistance. Similarly, relationships with friends and families are woven by the threads of entitlement. When these threads become frayed by unreasonable or unfounded expectations, or even by inherent imperfections, people sometimes mount wounding attacks on each other.

Potential entitlement issues arise in cases where one fallen being expects more than is possible from another, and conflicts result from such disregard of the flaws in ourselves and in others. I will tackle the entitlement issue from the perspective of 1) human to human interplay, 2) human interconnection with the Earth, and 3) human interaction with God. Somehow our expectations must mature enough to level with the reality that God is our Father and desires that we place total dependence on Him, not another fallen, imperfect being. Why strain our brothers and sisters with the demand for perfection? That expectation is conveniently and deceptively blasphemous, even idolatrous, and could be outright insensitive if not avoided by shrewd judgement.

We do not have to look too far or too hard to see the dependent relationship between husbands and wives, children and parents, congregants and pastors, patients and doctors, and students and teachers. Though most associate evil with Satan, and correctly so, why do so many still use God's name as a curse word to express anger, fear, or panic? We have all heard some say things like "Oh, Christ" or "Jesus Christ," and their intention is disrespectful. Why don't they say, "Oh, Satan"?

Day after day, Satan kills people with entitlement issues.

Somehow the world has forgotten that there is only a single source of life and that we are ultimately accountable to God alone. We perhaps no longer focus on the promise in Philippians 4:19 that reminds us that God alone can provide all our needs. Instead, we dash to the nearest human, closely biologically related or not, for a quick solution.

> *And my God will supply all your needs according to his riches in glory in Christ Jesus. (Philippians 4:19, CSB)*

When another fallen being or human cannot provide the solution we seek in a timely or practical way, we often turn to words and thoughts of displeasure or anger. This too often leaves both parties in anguish and the demons laughing. Indeed, parents are entitled to the respect of their children, employees should earn their wages with appropriate labor, professionals should be acclaimed for their skills, and favor should be doled out where merited. Still, proper expectation management should supervise such interplay.

Foremost, we must remember that the person you seek to cut down with criticism is furnished by the same life-source as you, made by the same hands as you, and is as faulty as you. If you were from a different universe, created and managed by another God, then perhaps you may be entitled to a prideful remark. But we cannot expect perfection from anyone. We must be wise enough to acknowledge that everyone is a test subject on Earth; if we were perfect, we would be in Heaven, not on Earth. Unchecked entitlement displeases God, because entitlement leads us to murmur and complain as feelings of impatience and superiority cloud sober reasoning. When we start to wholeheartedly place confidence in God alone, we begin to understand others at a level that causes us to respond to them with humility and a caring heart. We begin to see them as Jesus sees us: as children in need of help. Let's not burden others with undue accountability—help and support them and offer encouragement in the more challenging cases.

> **Therefore, we may boldly say, The Lord is my helper; I will not be afraid.** What can man do to me? (Hebrews 13:6, CSB)

> Rejoice in the Lord always; again I will say, rejoice. **Let your reasonableness be known to everyone.** The Lord is at hand. (Philippians 4:4-5, ESV)

> **Be merciful, just as your Father also is merciful.** (Luke 6:36, CSB)

The privilege and liberty to share thoughts, to be heard and respected, and to expect assistance from families and friends are entitlements that people retain to preserve hope and make life on Earth bearable. As noted above, issues arise when we demand perfection from imperfect beings. The entitlement consideration extends beyond human interaction. In some circles, the Earth is not only a place for mere mortals, but it is also a deity that they worship.

We have all heard the term "Mother Earth," a term that evokes notions of fertility, nurture, and a loving mother. In some religions, the same expression refers to the goddess of the Earth. In its most common understanding and personification, "Mother Earth" is recognized as the giver and sustainer of life. To indulge any thought that promotes the Earth as a life-giver is a harsh sentiment against our Creator, the true giver and sustainer of life. The Earth is animated by God-giving life, not vice versa. Understandably, there are many mesmerizing things on this planet, but they are presented to reflect the majesty of the Master of the Universe, not to receive reverence or reckless dependence. One might revere the Earth for its wonders and its provision of food and other comforts, but this is a foolhardy and idolatrous attempt to see the Earth as more than just a tool. God created this earthly dwelling to maintain the physical structure of His temple—the human body—as He places the soul through a battery of tests for a duration called a lifetime. That is the purpose of the Earth; it cannot owe you anything because it does not have life.

> *Jesus said to him, "I am the Way, the Truth, and the Life. (John 14:6, NKJV)*

Now let's look at how entitlement directly fits in with our relationship with God. The most life-threatening entitlement issue relates to one's eternal life. Each of us can live one of two lives. The first and more important life is lived by God's standards and is achieved when we make a wholehearted commitment to follow Christ until we expire from Earth. The second and less important life is one of carnality, a style of life that lives only for itself, not for God or for Heaven, and that takes the soul to Hell after it has run its course. For as long as a person lives, God is ever reaching out through His Spirit, trying to nudge each person toward His lifestyle. On the opposing side, the Devil tempts and lures us to his side through lustful and prideful enticements. Therein lies the problem. While indulging in the privilege of free will, human beings often feel entitled to pursue whatever offers the greatest gratification and sense of control.

Living as one pleases does give a sense of power and authority, an entitlement to a perceived self-power, coupled with the relative freedom to indulge in whatever quenches a natural, lustful appetite. However, what is deemed control and leeway to do as one pleases is only a test God has allowed or ordained.

The unwise or uninformed may still misconstrue it, even to their own detriment.

A lustful man pursuing a carnal or immoral life is similar to a drowning man clinging to a straw or a lifebuoy in stormy seas, while Jesus is nearby beckoning the one in peril to come into His boat. The shortsighted, perishing soul would reject the rescue attempt and instead grasp more tightly to the false hope of a self-directed life, failing to realize that the limited strength of such hope will soon be exhausted. We must recognize that perceived control is only a test of our trustworthiness. God is always challenging us to demonstrate whether we are faithful in the little things so that He can trust us with the big things. Life on Earth is a little thing because time is merely a breath or a wink compared to eternity. The message in Luke 16:10 can be interpreted as a question from God: if I can't trust you with the littleness of life on Earth, how can I entrust or entitle you with eternal matters?

> *He who is faithful in what is least is faithful also in much; and he who is unjust in what is least is unjust also in much. (Luke 16:10, NKJV)*

In a salesperson's terms, God is ultimately offering us a priceless gift; we are getting a spiritual bargain. Today, He extends His life to us to replace the false sense of safety that clutching to a straw provides. We must remember that He owns both the seas and straws. We must be willing to embrace the long-term perspective that both the seas and the straws will eventually pass away.

> *Long ago You [oh, Lord] established the earth, and the heavens are the work of Your hands. They will perish, but You [oh, Lord] will endure; all of them will wear out like clothing. You will change them*

> like a garment, and they will pass away. But You
> are the same, and Your years [oh, Lord] will never
> end. (Psalms 102:25-27, CSB)

Whatever grip you have on anything in this life will eventually fail, because neither you nor the thing you grasp extends beyond time, which in itself will ultimately cease to exist. We are not entitled to anything but the gift of salvation, because the Earth is already the Lord's.

> The earth is the LORD's, and all its fullness, The world
> and those who dwell therein. For He has founded it
> upon the seas, And established it upon the waters.
> (Psalms 24:1-2, NKJV)

> For I know the plans I have for you—this is the LORD's
> declaration—plans for your well-being, not for
> disaster, to give you a future and a hope. (Jeremiah
> 29:11, CSB)

THE PURPOSE OF TESTING
AN APPROACH TO CREATING VALUE

Testing is a procedure intended to establish the quality, performance, or reliability of something, especially before it is taken into widespread use.

> *In this you greatly rejoice, though now for a little while, if need be, you have been grieved by various trials, that the genuineness of your faith, being much more precious than gold that perishes, though it is tested by fire, may be found to praise, honor, and glory at the revelation of Jesus Christ. (1 Peter 1:6-7, NKJV)*

*P*erhaps you are reading this book on an electronic device, or perhaps in a printed format. Either way, both methods have this one thing in common: the equipment that produced them has undergone numerous tests to ensure that it produces marketable reading material. The purpose of such testing is to achieve a specific end or goal; after all, without knowing what you are testing for, how can you develop a meaningful testing plan, much less recognize the value or significance of any results? Among the many attributes of a test, the ones pertinent in this chapter are requirement, source, value, input, performance, cycle, and result. Testing dominates and permeates the domain of us mere mortals, us fallen beings, and is the investment strategy that God uses to "find" Heaven-ready souls. Testing is an approach to creating value from fallen beings.

> *Beloved, do not be surprised at the fiery trial when it comes upon you to test you, as though something strange were happening to you. But rejoice insofar as you share Christ's sufferings, that you may also rejoice and be glad when his glory is revealed. (1 Peter 4:12-13, ESV)*

In a testing environment for software or hardware, the operator does not ordinarily experience any physical or emotion impact from the test. However, when one is the direct target of the testing, a deeply subjective mindset descends to help us brace for its impact. Since Jesus came to redeem the soul from The Fall, His primary concern is placing the soul through a battery of tests to ready it for eternity. The approach He uses to fashion a person into an image of Himself may involve physical pain through sickness or injury, psychological uneasiness from disturbances in relationships, and spiritual challenges from the hordes of Hell. Why must life be so demanding and uncomfortable at times? The easy and accurate answer is that life is the road to perfection that we imperfect beings must take, and that each person has a uniquely challenging journey. Accepting this answer will enable us to set practical expectations. Life on Earth is not a picnic outing; it is a spiritual and business-oriented mission to rescue souls from falling into Hell. However, proper expectation management will help a soul to accept rather than struggle against testing.

> *I, the LORD, search the heart, I test the mind, Even to give every man according to his ways, According to the fruit of his doings. (Jeremiah 17:10, NKJV)*

The **requirement** to test humans is so critical that God, through Jesus, subjects Himself to suffering in the process. Though He ordains or allows the testing duration and conditions, His love for us causes Him to hurt whenever we suffer; He is not indifferent or uninvolved in our pains and suffering. The need for testing is built on a foundation of value. Your worth, my worth, and everyone's worth is not visible. Why? Because it is measured in God, the **source**: we are the likeness of the invisible, uncreated, self-existent God. Therefore, our souls, which are that image, are priceless. All the hardship in this world pales in comparison to the **value** of your life. Testing is required because the souls must take on the brilliance, the pure gold nature, of God to reenter Heaven. Therein lies the prerequisites for the refiner's fire, the crucible of transformation to remove the dross, as it were, from our life. God wants to give all observers on Earth and in Heaven an excellent **performance** of His patience, love, and faithfulness to sustain us through each testing **cycle**, irrespective of the type of **input** (lack, pain, torture, sorrow, tribulation) He allows in the testing process. Our lives are His anyway. Realizing that we have no other but God helps to achieve a successful **result**, a passing grade.

> ***Blessed is the one who endures trials***, *because when*

he has stood the test he will receive the crown of life that God has promised to those who love him. (James 1:12, CSB)

A crucible for silver, and a smelter for gold, and the LORD is the tester of hearts. (Proverbs 17:3, CSB)

Life is chock-full of tests. For instance, the transformative process that creates an adult butterfly is a test of strength and of determination to change from egg to larva, then for the larva to break through its inner protective chrysalis and outer silk-based cocoon into adulthood. Chrysalis is a 17th-century word with the Latin root *chrysallis* and the Ancient Greek root *khrusos*, meaning gold. God allows and ordains testing in order to turn us into pure gold. Each test is like a chrysalis or transitional state: we must either prove our determination to break out of it and to overcome it, or remain encased by it forever.

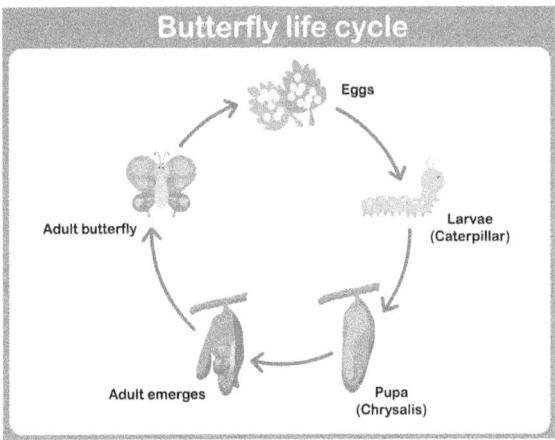

To be tested by God is a reality we must grapple with and welcome. If we live as though God will ensure smooth sailing all through this life and as though no aches or pains are allowed by

Him, then life will be all the more challenging due to our soul's foolhardy expectations. To that end, there are two significant aspects of a test: bracing oneself for its potential rigor, and having foreknowledge about it as a preparatory measure to bolster oneself mentally. The knowledge that, for instance, that the road ahead is uncrossable due to a rockslide or a deep chasm would remove the potential anxiety of an abrupt stop.

> *Dear brothers, is your life full of difficulties and temptations? Then be happy, for when the way is rough, your patience has a chance to grow. So let it grow, and don't try to squirm out of your problems. For when your patience is finally in full bloom, then you will be ready for anything, strong in character, full and complete. (James 1:2-4, TLB)*

Testing is a defensive mechanism that protects life, even our eternal life. When we drive on the highway, we visually test and maneuver our steering against collisions; we smell and visually inspect what we eat at a restaurant or gather from a supermarket; we test our friends and families for trustworthiness using verbal communication and body language. The examples can go on and on. Indeed, everything is a test of sorts. Some tests are structured like college exams and employment probation, while others are highly unstructured and even judgmental, such as a hesitation to give a homeless person a few dollars out of fear that your contribution might be misused. If we, as free-thinking, short-lived existences, invest so much in testing for our survival and comfort, should we not expect God to do the same from an eternal perspective?

> *We also rejoice in our afflictions, because we know that affliction produces endurance, endurance produces*

> *proven character, and proven character produces hope. This hope will not disappoint us, because God's love has been poured out in our hearts through the Holy Spirit who was given to us.*
> *(Romans 5:3-5, CSB)*

Life on Earth is, in its entirety, the test of tests. Each exam result is a preview of either Heaven or Hell. Heaven observes how people interplay: are they selfish, or are they caring and sharing? Do they live peaceably with each other, or are they quarrelsome? God inspects our lives and selects those who demonstrate love and friendship toward Him and others, those who are suitable for Heaven.

> *In this you rejoice, though now for a little while, if necessary, you have been grieved by various trials, so that the tested genuineness of your faith—more precious than gold that perishes though it is tested by fire—may be found to result in praise and glory and honor at the revelation of Jesus Christ. (1 Peter 1:6-7, ESV)*

People are on Earth today because God is not ready to usher them back into Heaven, possibly due to an unfinished mission or even an uncompleted test. Some are waiting, literally queued up, for eternal separation from Him unless they repent. Still, both types of souls will be tested or tempted to improve themselves, to help others, or both. God loves them all equally, but people make their own lifestyle decisions. Each person plays only a role in the single body of God, His creation. One member's operation in any given instance of time may not be intended for itself only. For example, the hand is part of the body, but taking food from a plate to the mouth does not provide the hand pleasure, but only the soul through the tastebuds. Still, the hand is not a second fiddle in this orchestration of nutritional intake.

Now that we are aware that testing is mandatory due to our imperfection, let's embrace it, not fight it by murmuring or complaining. Such a struggle is futile and displeases God, who wants to prepare us to reenter Heaven once we have overcome the challenges that mercilessly and unrelentingly lure us toward Hell.

> *The Lord knows how to rescue the godly from trials and to keep the unrighteous under punishment for the day of judgment, especially those who follow the polluting desires of the flesh and despise authority. (2 Peter 2:9-10, CSB)*

> *But may the God of all grace, who called us to His eternal glory by Christ Jesus, after you have suffered a while, perfect, establish, strengthen, and settle you. To Him be the glory and the dominion forever and ever. Amen. (1 Peter 5:10-11, NKJV)*

WHY WE SHOULD PRAY
WE ARE NOT PERFECT

Pray without ceasing, in everything give thanks; for this is the will of God in Christ Jesus for you. (1 Thessalonians 5:17-18, NKJV)

Why should we pray? Why is prayer mandatory even though God does not enforce it? Because of free will – one of God's universal laws or terms of engagement - He would not forcefully demand prayer. However, were we perfect, there would be no need to pray; instead, we would only need to offer praise and thanks. Perhaps that is all the angels do in Heaven. However, we are imperfect and have an enormous appetite for wrongdoing. Many do not realize that sin violates God's standards for holiness, and each transgression grants the enemy permission to attack and control us until we are rescued through repentance. We must ask for divine help. Otherwise, we may suffer various losses, and even physical and spiritual death.

A transgression is equivalent to selling a part of oneself to the enemy and rendering one's soul incomplete. A person with an incomplete soul is broken; one cannot reenter Heaven in that condition. Prayers are needed, therefore, to purge us of poisonous consumption, reclaim the missing pieces of our soul, and make ourselves whole again.

Without a supernatural intervention in response to our prayers, we will irreversibly decay. Not readily seeing the soul's decay is part of the deception that lures us to sin. The necessity for cleansing and wellness in turn indicates the requirement for prayer. We die if we do not pray, because we consume spiritual poison every day through our thoughts and deeds and we therefore must pray without ceasing.

We pray for wisdom and discernment to peacefully and reasonably live with families and others. For example, when coworkers, neighbors, or even pedestrians obstruct the peace of your routine, it is easy to see them as the enemy. Retaliating with harsh words of criticism and condemnation can seem like a quick and satisfying solution as you strive to regain a peaceful state of being and fend off the threat. Other times, your response might be a professional or courteous smile, an attempt to hide any deep-seated anger and to portray yourself as friendly, despite your unpleasant thoughts. However, social conflict can sink to a much lower level when emotions boil within the home, when the hordes of Hell, as it appears, have entered the house as visible commanders. How do you handle those conditions in a God-fearing and genuinely human-friendly way? How do we cope when those closest to us have become emotionally violent or combative? Do we lose hope and prosecute and blame them? No. We pray.

We pray to understand how God controls our lives by allowing and ordaining certain events, pleasant and unpleasant, as we see in Isaiah 45:7:

> "I form the light and create darkness, I make peace and create calamity; I, the LORD, do all these things."
> (Isaiah 45:7, NKJV)

We must not fall victim to the temptation to hold resentments and grudges over thoughts such as "My sister or brother did me wrong. My father or mother did not act parentally sound--how could my own family treat me in that way? I would understand if they were outsiders." In a way, we are all outsiders, because we are all fallen beings whom God has placed in specific family-oriented settings to help us mature and make us ready to return to Heaven. When we blame others, we unknowingly promote them over God in the situation, responding to them as though they are in control. All the while, Heaven is trying to nudge us toward the truth that everything is the working of God, that nothing happens unless He signs off on it.

We must keep in mind that God always wants the best for us, but that, like good medicine, His plan may not always taste pleasant; by the way, God does not owe us anything. We also must appreciate and acknowledge the law of sowing and reaping that God has instituted on Earth. We are directly responsible for some of the tough lessons in life. Let's look beyond the small picture of mortal existence and interplay and behold the big view of God's perfect will and love working to help you to reenter Heaven. Do not become distracted by your physical body's earthly placement and arrangements; it is all a stage anyway. Pray and perform well. God and angels are watching. Cope with the distractions; they are there to help you manage your life and time. Use them to your advantage--time is running out.

> *I form the light and make the dark.* ***I send good times and bad.*** *I, Jehovah, am he who does these things [to help you]. (Isaiah 45:7, TLB)*

> *I form light and create darkness,* ***I make success and create disaster;*** *I am the LORD, who does all these things [to help you]. (Isaiah 45:7, CSB)*

> *I form light and create darkness;* ***I make well-being and create calamity;*** *I am the LORD, who does all these things [to help you]. (Isaiah 45:7, ESV)*

> — THREE TRANSLATIONS OF ISAIAH 45:7

LIFE-SAVING QUESTIONS
ANSWER WITH THE END IN MIND

A sensible person sees danger and takes cover, but the inexperienced keep going and are punished. (Proverbs 22:3, CSB)

1. If you are not in right-standing with God, then examine your choices closely: do you realize that billions just like you have died and are not in Heaven?
2. The Bible teaches that God lives in and through all things, including you and me. Do you believe that He

is in you at this moment? If so, are you doing anything to offend Him?
3. While our bodies do eventually die, our souls live forever. Where beyond Earth do you want to live when your body has left you—there are only two options: Heaven or Hell?
4. The only place where we can continue our relationship with loved ones is in Heaven; what are you willing to do to avoid forever living in a friendless world of total isolation and terror?
5. Like the story about the talents in the Bible, every breath is God's investment in a soul. How are you managing His investment in you? Are you using it for good or for evil? Are you turning it into a profit for His kingdom by doing things acceptable in His sight, or are you doing things to promote the kingdom of darkness?
6. Everything we do needs life or energy; therefore, we cannot do anything without Him; He is Life. That said, God is the first investor, and like us when we invest (in our finances, education, and business), He expects a profit. After all, we are made in His likeness. Do you know that each of us will give Him, He the most mission-focus investor, an account of how we spent His life and time?
7. God requires that each of us spend our fleeting days attending to His requirements for holiness. Each soul or person has just enough time to complete His requests. Do you think He wants you to be engrossed, through gossiping, backstabbing, hatred, or grudges, in what He does in the life of another person?
8. God is the most loving and caring person. Yes, He is a real person with an infinite passion for righteousness, but you must know that He also has a passion for

judgment, for justice. Would He not, then, dispense His wrath against unprofitable souls (those living in disobedience)?
9. In the eyes of God, wisdom is living an obedient life, while foolishness is following the path of rebellion or disobedience. Would you like to be called a fool? Wouldn't you prefer to be named amongst the wise and profitable servants or children of God?
10. Remember, Jesus did not die for anything material or visible from the Earth. We are aliens on the Earth because our souls, our real selves, are invisible and not of Earth. Our bodies are transient, material, fleeting things, but don't you know that He died for your soul, which is His image?
11. Satan and demons don't have free will; we do. We choose good over evil, accept or reject God, and live as we please to the extent that God allows. What can the Devil choose? He is already perfectly evil. What would God want to choose? He is already perfect in goodness; moreover, He cannot change. Do you know that after or near death, free will is revoked, we enter eternity, and we forever become what we have been choosing or fashioning all our lives?
12. There is no love in Hell because God is Love. Do you know that there is no friendly communication or interaction in Hell, only hatred and bitter regrets?
13. If you live contrary to God, do you realize the most valuable use of today is as an opportunity to repent (to change) and to avoid the eternal inferno that is now the forever-home of billions?
14. You are more important than everything on Earth combined. Why? Because the life of Christ is priceless. Have you considered that your life is just as important to God as Jesus's is to Him? You are more

valuable than you can ever imagine; however, your true value is in Christ. Why? Because through Christ, we become perfect, and perfection is the requirement to reenter Heaven.

> *If you want to know what God wants you to do, ask him, and he will gladly tell you, for He is always ready to give a bountiful supply of wisdom to all who ask Him; He will not resent it." (James 1:5, TLB)*

PROMISE WITH UNDERSTANDING
A POTENTIAL TRAP BY PASSION

It is irresponsible to make an oath without understanding its ramification and impact.

> *Death and life are in the power of the tongue [in speaking], and those who love it will eat its fruit.*
> *(Proverbs 18:21, CSB)*

By definition, an oath is a solemn promise, a sworn statement that often invokes a divine witness, perhaps God or Jesus, with a passionate vision toward one's future action or behavior. The enthusiasm to escape a discomforting or displeasing event and the fervent hope for abstinence from it are the driving forces that inspire someone to commit wholeheartedly to a change, to make a promise. The promiser is so enthralled by the prospect of newness and of perceived dependability that they become engulfed by a mental utopia in which a promised better version of their future self presumably exists. The challenge of a pledge lies in reaching and maintaining this idealistic state to avoid a relapse.

> **Better that you do not vow than that you vow and not fulfill it.** *Do not let your mouth bring guilt on you, and do not say in the presence of the messenger that it was a mistake. Why should God be angry with your words and destroy the work of your hands?* (Ecclesiastes 5:5-6, CSB)

The desire to demonstrate reliability or trustworthiness is pleasing to both God and our fellow Earth citizens. However, it is a familiar and true statement that the road to Hell is paved with good intentions. A promise should not be mentally constructed or actively construed as merely a good faith attempt or a gesture of willingness that anyone should accept. Instead, a promise must be understood and conveyed as an explicit or implicit agreement to deliver what was promised. Until a potential promiser has come to terms with that understanding, it is best to stay clear of any binding agreements, verbally or written, socially or otherwise. Why? Because a failed promise is the mismanagement of words and the incomplete understanding of their potential impact.

In the beginning, God spoke the world into existence, and He is still speaking today to and through His images—images that include you and me. As a result, our words are also powerful and consequential. Evidence of this is shown in Matthew 12:36-37, Mark 11:23, and Ecclesiastes 5:5-6. Why? Anything we do uses energy or life; He is the Life through His

Spirit. We are responsible for how we use His strength in all forms of communication and interactions. We are even warned in Ecclesiastes 5:2 to keep our words be to a minimum, to avoid foolishness or sin.

> *For assuredly, I say to you,* **whoever says to this mountain, 'Be removed and be cast into the sea,'** *and does not doubt in his heart, but believes that those things he says will be done, he will have whatever he says.* (Mark 11:23, NKJV)

> *But I say to you that* **for every idle word men may speak, they will give account of it in the day of judgment.** *For by your words you will be justified, and by your words you will be condemned.* (Matthew 12:36-37, NKJV)

> **Do not be rash with your mouth,** *and let not your heart utter anything hastily before God. For God is in heaven, and you on earth; Therefore let your words be few.* (Ecclesiastes 5:2, NKJV)

Making a promise and neglecting to fulfill it is spiritually dangerous and a possible entrapment set by demons to rob people of God's blessings. I can think of two scenarios: 1) Losing a case in the spiritual courtroom, and 2) reliance on self.

Comparable to Ecclesiastes 5:2 and Matthew 12:36-37 is what is called the Miranda warning or Miranda rights in the United States: a notification required to be given by police to criminal suspects, advising them of their right to silence even under questioning by law enforcement officials. Offering Too Much Information (TMI) can be potentially harmful to a suspect, so it's advisable that they think long and hard about anything they say. Similarly, without considering its cost and impact, making a promise is volunteering too much information, even idly speaking. Communication management is critical to harmony. Moreover, when we make promises to God and others, demons are actively taking notes. Failure to adhere to the terms of the promise can grant the enemy the justification to challenge or accuse us before God. We could legally suffer if we don't ask for forgiveness or if we ignore the promise due to a memory lapse. Therefore, always write down your promises and manage them closely. If you fail in any, go to God immediately and defend yourself with a plea for forgiveness. Do not let your tongue cause you to stumble and suffer. Proverbs 18:21 and James 3:5 warn that we can either ensure life or cause death based on what we say.

> *So also the tongue is a small member, yet it boasts of great things. How great a forest is set ablaze by such a small fire! (James 3:5, ESV)*

> *The accuser of our brethren, who accused them before our God day and night, has been cast down. (Revelation 12:10, NKJV)*

Too often, when we make a promise, we consider only our perceived capabilities, either materially or physically. Frequently, I would argue, not even an inkling of thought is given to God's strength or will. Instead, we boast about our imperfection and become deceived by our pride, even if unintentionally. Zechariah 4:6 and James 4:14-16 guide us on how we should approach a promise.

> *This is the word of the LORD to Zerubbabel: '**Not by strength or by might, but by my Spirit**,' says the LORD of Armies. (Zechariah 4:6, CSB)*

*Yet you do not know what tomorrow will bring—what your life will be! For you are like vapor that appears for a little while, then vanishes. Instead, you should say, **"If the Lord wills, we will live and do this or that**.*" *But as it is, you boast in your arrogance. All such boasting is evil. (James 4:14-16, CSB)*

Make a promise if you may, but don't forget about God. Consider Him before you commit to any promise.

Commit thy way unto the LORD; trust also in him; and He shall bring it to pass. (Psalms 37:5, KJV)

THE REBIRTH OF A FALLEN BEING
CREATING A HEAVEN-READY SOUL

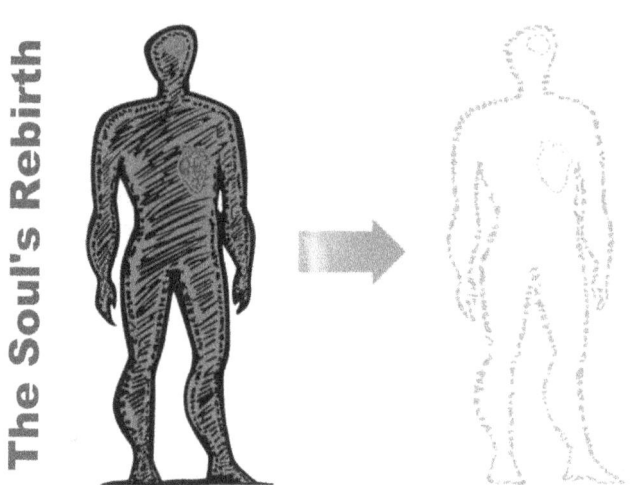

The Soul's Rebirth

| Changing from darkness to light through the fire of God's Spirit.

> *And you He made alive, who were dead in trespasses and sins, in which you once walked according to the course of this world, according to the prince of the power of the air, the spirit who now works in the sons of disobedience, among whom also we all once*

conducted ourselves in the lusts of our flesh, fulfilling the desires of the flesh and of the mind, and were by nature children of wrath, just as the others. (Ephesians 2:1-3, NKJV)

This guide is filled with numerous references to "fallen beings," but have you ever asked yourself from where we have fallen? The most direct answer is Heaven. We are no longer with heavenly angels, and no one can return to Heaven until a spiritual rebirth. So, for example, unless a child dies before its first transgression, that is before it gets a chance to use free will against God, it is practically in the same predicament as any other unrepentant soul: as yet unready to stand before God until they repent and turn to Jesus. The descent to Earth is not as wonderful as some may believe, because visible things do not reflect even an inch of the value of a soul. Unless your soul is in good standing with God, which is the only passport issued by Heaven for reentry, only eternal woes await. I am just as serious about this point as I am about other calls to repentance in this volume. God loves us and desires a reunion, but He has an unresolved, eternal issue with unrepented sins. A rebirth is required to profitably run the race against constantly depleting time.

Humans are not expected to spend their lives indulging in fantasies, spoiling themselves off of the land, or idling away the hours on mortal pleasures, but rather to use our time to realize this truth: that we are at war with a gang of diabolical ancient beasts. The invisible, dark army, formerly from the bliss of Heaven, continues to operate today in accordance with a mission and a mandate to destroy all those whom God has blessed with the opportunity of reentering Heaven; you and I are included in this list, and we must fight like "hell" to return home. In fact, we must become even better warriors than our opponents. This is a grave matter; the condition of our eternity depends on this truth. More than anything physical, we are spiritual aliens on Earth; this place is not our home. We are from eternity and we are heading back to God, day by day. Let us prepare to meet Him.

Rebirth, in this context, as might be expected, is not about reincarnation, which refers to being reborn in another body. Instead, rebirth is about restoration and a new beginning for the soul. Why a new beginning? Any being that has fallen or has been expelled from Heaven, expelled from the presence of Life (Jesus), dies spiritually and must be resuscitated by rebirth. The soul must be brought back to life by the Spirit, because nothing dead can return to Heaven. We walk or run to Heaven on the narrowest of paths; we are not brought there. Rebirth is not a one-time event. It begins at repentance and requires constant maintenance.

The most essential and challenging lesson we learn is the one that teaches how to happily take second or last place in everything, thereby putting God in the first position. This divine, lifelong tutoring is part of the rebirthing process that enables a soul to love like Jesus loves and prepares it to reenter Heaven. Outside of this undertaking are only needless frustrations and various inefficiencies spanning the visible and the invisible, the body and the soul. Do not fight God for the helm in your life; you will lose every time. Work with Him instead, because everyone is already too busy working on themselves with hardly anything to spare. Moreover, the path for each soul is not wide enough to accommodate another; God engineered your path for you alone to avoid distraction and contention.

Nevertheless, there is excellent news. We have hope because of one word: love. Admittedly, I was once one of those folks who believes that God is touchy and becomes irritable at every transgression. The opposite, though, does not promote the notion that God overlooks any sin, as that would be quite silly. Instead, let us read about love in 1 Corinthians 13:4-8 before I proceed any further: "Love is patient, love is kind, it is not jealous; love does not brag, it is not arrogant. It does not act disgracefully, it does not seek its own benefit; it is not provoked, does not keep an account of a wrong suffered, it does not rejoice in unrighteousness, but rejoices with the truth; it keeps every confidence, it believes all things, hopes all things, endures all things. Love never fails." These informative and corrective verses detail the hope mentioned earlier. The love that Christ has for us is a lifelong invitation to come to Him unashamed, with an attitude of repentance, knowing you are appreciated and endlessly loved.

A Pharisee named Nicodemus had questions about the process of rebirth. Jesus explained to Him that the transformation was primarily spiritual, followed by a godly lifestyle. Everyone, until repentance, is a Nicodemus of sorts. Perhaps owing to some oversight in reasoning or perhaps to plain pride, we have not dealt with the question of salvation, which is our spiritual permit to Heaven and evidence of our rebirth. We will fly away one day, so get your travel documents in order today because tomorrow is promised to no one.

> There was a man of the Pharisees named Nicodemus, a ruler of the Jews. This man came to Jesus by night and said to Him, "Rabbi, we know that You are a teacher come from God; for no one can do these signs that You do unless God is with him." Jesus answered and said to him, "Most assuredly, I say to you, unless one is born again, he cannot see the kingdom of God." Nicodemus said to Him, "How can a man be born when he is old? Can he enter a second time into his mother's womb and be born?" Jesus answered, "Most assuredly, I say to you, unless one is born of water and the Spirit, he cannot enter the kingdom of God. That which is born of the flesh

> is flesh, and that which is born of the Spirit is spirit." (John 3:1-6, NKJV)

MY EXPERIENCES AND OBSERVATIONS

1. Everyone is from eternity, the home of spirits. Each soul is a spirit. There are two aspects of the invisible realm of spirits: a marvelous light called Heaven and terrifying darkness known as Hell. Unlike our bodies, our souls do not reside in any physical domain but rather in eternity, even while interacting with others. Now, given the fact that immortality has two sides, ask yourself: which one currently holds my soul? Heaven or Hell? This is a vital question. Jude 1:23 answers by stating that those still pursuing unrepentance are already in the inferno and must be "snatched from the very flames of Hell itself". You would be remiss to take this statement figuratively: John (the author) is quite serious and literal about this warning. A person not in good standing with God is already in Hell, while the upright are in heavenly places. "We sit with Him in the heavenly realms—all because of what Christ Jesus did" (Ephesians 2:6). These scriptural accounts indicate that a person, during their life on Earth, is already situated in eternity. Why? Because no one can decide about eternal life after death. Only the living have the free will to make this decision.
2. It is unwise to engage in envy or coveting. Not even the most pious Christian is worthy of that level of admiration. Why? Because until a person dies and reenters Heaven, we are all still in the same boat, and no one's position is assured—no one knows the final

state of a person's life. Every day, some people turn to Christ while others backslide. This statement is not meant to be disrespectful or to discount anyone's efforts toward holiness. It merely seeks to defend the truth that Jesus is our model and that we ceaselessly strive to become like Him. For example, when a spiritual leader falls from grace, that event should not evoke more than prayers for the wounded soul or soldier. No one is suitable for condemnation. Always consider that a failure in any one person demonstrates the potentiality of failure in another.

3. The physical world cannot provide the soul's needs; mortal hands cannot satisfy its hunger nor quench its thirst. Our fanciest restaurants and most luxurious offerings are distasteful to the soul, because the material cannot quench spiritual desires. Otherwise, the rich would have a reasonable chance of getting back to Heaven on account of wealth. Fortunately, God is entirely spiritual.

4. Life is more than the pain we feel, more than the sporadic moments of joy, our ambitions for tomorrow, or the grudges we release or hoard. It is more than the thrill of victory and the agony of defeat, our beliefs and doubts, whom we respect or disregard, or our lacks or surpluses. Life on Earth is about dying to obtain spiritual rebirth. Many souls fail to reenter Heaven, because they refuse to willfully die. Until the soul sheds its Adamic, self-driven nature, it continues to fight God for self-rule, but He will not contend with mere mortals for the liberty that He granted them through the gift of the power to choose.

5. A fallen being is stained and disfigured by sin, though the outward appearance of such beings may

sometimes hint otherwise. As a result, it is often a painful process to fashion such a being back into the glorious image of God. Everyone, I presume, wants to reenter Heaven, yet hardly anyone welcomes the refining process.

6. As I continue to think about life, I find it more and more disruptive to murmur and complain. Why? How could a fallen being become disgruntled before the humble and perfectly loving Creator? How rude and prideful can imperfection be? Humans are so easily deceived and so inflated with the fumes of conceit and vanity that we often lose focus on common spiritual sense. May God help us to understand ourselves and recognize the truth about our fallen state.

7. As a fallen being with a natural inclination to perform selfishly, kindness is extraordinary. Kindness is about "going the extra mile" to demonstrate the kind of sympathy typical of Jesus. This extra effort often requires the obedience and patience needed to "step into another's shoes" with compassion.

8. It is wondrous and precious to walk with Jesus. Abstaining from sin in thoughts and deeds cleanses one. I sincerely desire that lifestyle, but, as with any success, maintenance is not optional for its upkeep. In my experience, laziness, complacency, indiscipline, and inconsistency represent more than the foxes that spoil the vines. These traits can destroy the owner or orchardist. The wise Solomon issues an alert in Song of Solomon 2:15: "Catch the foxes for us, the little foxes that are ruining the vineyards, while our vineyards are in blossom." Many of us have an inherent tendency to lean into complacency. If that attitude is left unchecked, then indiscipline and

inconsistency will promote a slow fade back into darkness, a fading which demands even more effort to overcome.

9. The outgrowth of one's rebirth is exuberance, as this process is bursting with the light of holiness. God is the Light; we too are lights with the Spirit as our energy source. Combined, we are the lights of the world. We shine through the ways in which we speak, dress, and interact with others. Remember, our observers cannot see what is in our hearts or souls, only what we express to their senses. In John 8:12, Jesus says, "**I am the Light of the world**; the one who follows Me will not walk in the darkness, but will have the Light of life." However, we are His hands and feet—active members of His body. Matthew 5:14-16 describes the importance of our roles: "**You are the light of the world**. A city set on a hill cannot be hidden; nor do people light a lamp and put it under a basket, but on the lamp-stand, and it gives light to all who are in the house. Your light must shine before people in such a way that they may see your good works, and glorify your Father who is in Heaven." We must allow God, through His Spirit, to shine through us, eternally bright.

10. Let us come to terms with the reality that every life is an intellectual, spiritual, and physical connection point that joins and interacts with others, just as computers operate as part of a network. When we ignore God's prompts for service, either as a passthrough request or to perform an activity, we block or hinder Him, which is sinful.

11. When we effectively understand the gift of salvation and the need for it, our perspectives undergo a radical and immediate change. Until then, we are in "I" mode,

which is a masterful demonstration of pride, inefficiency, a dying soul. We must ask Jesus to help us switch from that destructive state to "His" mode. We must remember that we are the sheep, not the shepherds.

12. Our perspective on life must mirror the expectations presented in Matthew 10:34-37: "Don't imagine that I came to bring peace to the Earth! No, rather, a sword. I have come to set a man against his father, and a daughter against her mother, and a daughter-in-law against her mother-in-law—a man's worst enemies will be right in his own home! If you love your father and mother more than you love me, you are not worthy of being mine, or if you love your son or daughter more than me, you are not worthy of being mine." God is the prince of peace, but nothing can come before Him. He will not tolerate idolatry, which is darkness.
13. As we transform more and more into the nature of Christ, our questions will change from "Why?" to "How?" Instead of asking why something is or is not happening, we ask how we can fix our side. We must become assured in the truth that we are fallen beings in need of help.
14. Some believers like to talk about the number of hours they spend with God. However, instead of touting our time sacrificed to get up in the wee hours to pray, we should express gratitude for the privilege to do so and effectively realize we can do nothing without God, so all praises are unto Him.
15. When we understand what is at stake in our fallen state, we shift from complaining to giving thanks for all things. However, only the Spirit can perform this

transformation, so we ask God for His power: the Holy Spirit.
16. When we genuinely trust in the truth that God is more willing to give than we are to receive, we stop approaching Him with an attitude of questioning and impatience. He is not hiding from us; He wants to help. The nature of love is to share and give, so imagine what His perfect love can and will do.
17. Giving God merely a "doggie bag", or our leftover time, is not enough for rebirth. We must allocate more time for our spiritual growth. Increase devotion from 10 minutes to 20 to 30 to one or more hours at a time.
18. Unfriending pride (or self-service) and befriending service to God and others is one of the best ways to demonstrate patience and love.
19. We must become the seed described in John 12:24 by preparing ourselves to bear fruit: "Truly, truly I say to you, unless a grain of wheat falls into the Earth and dies, it remains alone; but if it dies, it bears much fruit". This process is one of time, solitude, and self-denial. It is about pursuing and experiencing the death of carnality, thereby allowing a substantial measure of His Spirit in one's life. His presence is power and life. It is about becoming the vessel or channel He needs in order to work through us, which is profitable and efficient stewardship.
20. When a soul matures to the extent that Joseph demonstrated in Genesis 39:9, I am sure God smiles. In this scenario, Potiphar's wife tried to seduce Joseph into sexual sin. Instead of giving in to this temptation, Joseph exclaimed, "How then can I do this great wickedness, and sin against God?" That is the level of

loyalty and self-denial that Heaven seeks from us earthlings.
21. Jesus is the Father in every prodigal situation. Each day, He lovingly waits for His wayward child to break the distant horizon, so that He can welcome him or her with a royal garment.
22. I usually spend my time with God on my knees. In my experience, it is more respectful, especially when I can do so physically. If I am too tired to attend devotion in my preferred posture, I find that God is more accepting of a few minutes on my knees than in my bed (assuming I am not sick). He is the King of kings and does not approve of laziness or subpar efforts.
23. Often, God waits for us, not the other way around. If He never waits, then the concept of "time running out" is void. We change over time, but He does not. At other times, though, He needs us to wait for Him, because there are seven billion of us in the world. He sometimes must wait for others to integrate them into a plan, which is all the more reason to make strategic prayers for each other in order to help bring others up to speed.
24. Never feel special or unique among God's children, as such feelings only lead to the deception known as pride. God does not have any favorites. He loves everyone equally, because His love is constant; it cannot increase or decrease.
25. A story in 2 Peter 2:22 tells of two mindsets, or double-mindedness (see James 1:8). The account is about a dog which returns to its vomit and a pig to its wallowing. Both Lot's wife and the Israelites (who were freed from Egyptian slavery), among others, had difficulty staying on the narrow path. They wanted to turn back or take a different route. Backsliding is

dangerous because, as the term infers, it moves the soul backward, possibly into Hell and beyond the reach of timely recovery. We cannot slide *back* into Heaven. Whether or not the pig and dog examples are in the Bible because their DNA are closely related to humans, the essence of the stories is about steadfastness in decision-making. God says we are either for Him or against Him (Matthew 12:30 and Matthew 6:24). The lesson and warning are about making a decision and sticking with it. Often, anxiety and uncertainty arise if we are not thankful and patient. We are so busy being unsatisfied with what we have that we are constantly chasing something more. We become frantic and overwhelmed, trying to fill the soul, a container of infinite capacity. Therein lies the insanity. I believe it is greed or a perceived feeling of lacking that causes souls to become disheartened and to eventually be lured back into darkness by diabolic beings with something akin to fool's gold. Joshua 24:15 sums up the lesson of 2 Peter 2:22: "Choose you this day whom ye will serve". I reckon that it is discontent that caused the dog to return to what it had previously renounced in a scornful expulsion.

26. Discontentment (murmur, complaints) is a generalized misunderstanding of the Earth-based, last-chance opportunity to prove or demonstrate to God, to Jesus, that we are serious about wanting to reenter Heaven after having entered into a fallen state. We like to joke around, but the life of Christ is no laughing matter. It is eternally momentous.

WORK OUT YOUR OWN SALVATION WITH FEAR AND TREMBLING

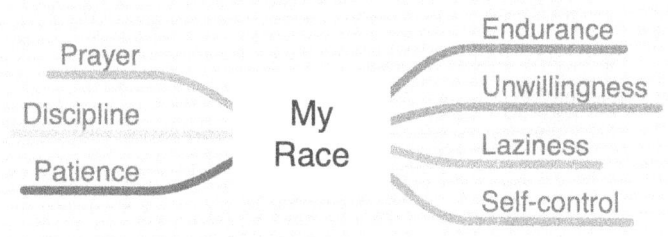

These are areas where I must apply more focus. Create a plan for yourself.

I have always heard that talk is cheap, and I'll say the same for righteous desires that never lead to any action. Nearly all of us concoct and pursue a New Year's resolution or two. Often, as you know, the main challenge we face is consistency: we usually fall off the bandwagon within a week or two of New Year's Day. Somewhere along the way, we lose focus. Laziness creeps in as endurance and discipline wane, and impatience claims victory. I am sure everyone in Hell has a similar story to tell, but it is too late for them. Getting back to

Heaven is more challenging and more consequential than any plan for physical health; after all, the body does not leave the Earth, anyway. It is the *soul* which can reach the highest places. I wish to provide you a list of areas that *I* myself hope to work on. Modify and personalize this list to your needs — make it your own. Make a plan.

1. **Prayer:** Rejoice always, pray without ceasing, in everything give thanks; for this is the will of God in Christ Jesus for you. Do not quench the Spirit. (1 Thessalonians 5:16-19, NKJV)
2. **Discipline (self-control):** Therefore we also, since we are surrounded by so great a cloud of witnesses, let us lay aside every weight, and the sin which so easily ensnares us, and let us run with endurance the race that is set before us. (Hebrews 12:1, NKJV) Harsh discipline is for him who forsakes the way, And he who hates correction will die. (Proverbs 15:10, NKJV)
3. **Patience (endurance):** And let us not grow weary while doing good, for in due season we shall reap if we do not lose heart. (Galatians 6:9, NKJV) And not only that, but we also glory in tribulations, knowing that tribulation produces perseverance and perseverance, character; and character, hope. (Romans 5:3-4, NKJV)
4. **Laziness (unwillingness):** The soul of a lazy man desires, and has nothing, but the soul of the diligent shall be made rich. (Proverbs 13:4, NKJV) "The lazy man will not plow because of winter; He will beg during harvest and have nothing. (Proverbs 20:4, NKJV)

Therefore, my beloved, as you have always obeyed, not as in my presence only, but now much more in my absence, **work out your own salvation with fear and trembling,** *for it is God who works in you both to will and to do for His good pleasure. (Philippians 2:12-13, NKJV)*

CREATE A SCHEDULE

Some people don't need a schedule. Some people seem to have an internal planner that supports a disciplined lifestyle, so they can remain dedicated to prioritizing tasks properly. Others, like myself, may need a detailed task list and a good dose of discipline to remain focused. Whatever kind of person you are, everyone needs to develop an attitude of determination. Some time ago, I heard someone say that a soldier needs endurance more than courage to survive. We are all spiritual warriors, so fight with your desired end in mind.

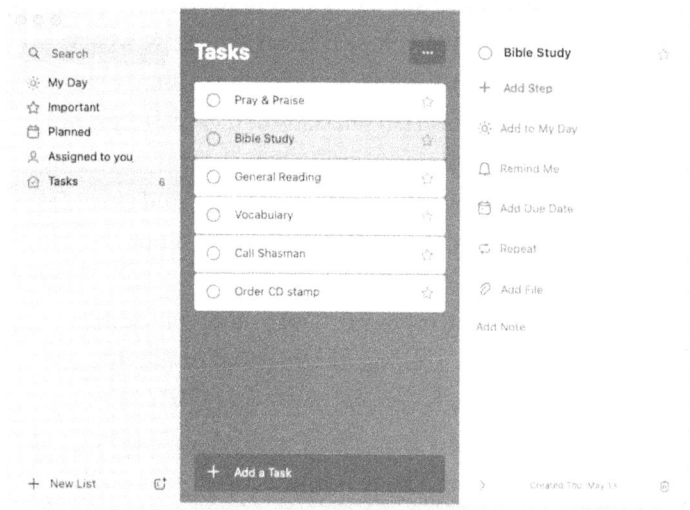

| Create a schedule and prioritize your time with God.

Including time for God in your schedule, I am sure, will

bring a smile to His face. He is jealous of our time: "For the LORD, whose name is Jealous, is a jealous God," (Exodus 34:14). If we don't spend time with Him, we are more than likely to drift off the narrow path to Heaven into a foreign world where only darkness and doom await.

> *But God shows His anger from Heaven against all sinful, evil men who push away the truth from them. (Romans 1:18, TLB)*

> *But no, you won't listen, and so you are saving up terrible punishment for yourselves because of your stubbornness in refusing to turn from your sin; for there is going to come a day of wrath when God will be the just Judge of all the world. (Romans 2:5, TLB)*

TRUST GOD TO HELP YOU

If you believe the Bible is the word of God, then you also acknowledge that it is the book of truths. Despite our imperfections and our fallen nature, humans generally dislike dishonesty; we are instinctively repelled by liars. In Numbers 23:19, we read that "God is not man, that He should lie, or a son of man, that He should change His mind. Has He said, and will He not do it? Or has He spoken, and will He not fulfill it?" Every good thought and deed is from Him. With that recognition, we can appreciate God's faithfulness to His promises and to all that He has spoken. If we couldn't trust God, then we would be better than Him, because He would be the chief of falsehood, and Satan would be His deputy, as it were. Therefore, realize that God does not mince words; He means what He says. We sometimes reject or shirk from promises because we fear a consequence or fear that we will be unable to fulfill that promise. God does not fear anyone nor will He ever be unable to fulfill His word. So join me in diving into the sea of confidence in Him.

> *You are of your father the devil, and the desires of your father you want to do. He was a murderer from the beginning, and does not stand in the truth, because there is no truth in him. When he speaks a lie, he speaks from his own resources, for he is a liar and the father of it. But because I tell the truth, you do not believe Me. (John 8:44-45, NKJV)*

ONLY PERFECTION ENTERS HEAVEN
WE MUST BECOME PERFECT

*His lord said unto him, **well done, thou good and faithful servant**: thou hast been faithful over a few things, I will make thee ruler over many things: enter thou into the joy of thy lord. (Matthew 25:21, KJV)*

*W*illiam and Robert Chambers were the first publishers of the Chamber's English Dictionary back in 1872. They define perfection as an event "done thoroughly or completely," "exactly conforming to definition or theory," "having every moral excellence," and "without flaw, blemish or fault." Only a perfect soul reenters Heaven. How, then, do we account for the familiar psychological and emotional haven created by the common adage "I am only human; I am not perfect"? The first half of that statement is true, but in this chapter, I will shed light on the last part, because we frequently do perform perfectly in various ways, but according to which or whose standards do we measure this perfection? Perfection is like hitting the bullseye of a dartboard, but whose board are you aiming at? Is it God's?

Imperfection can be very costly. On a supernatural level, Hell is full of billions of lives that were lived imperfectly and failed the standard for Heaven. Though many of them, I am sure, were moral people, they did not clothe themselves with the righteousness and perfection that only Jesus can provide. In other words, they did not have a perfect relationship with God through Jesus. To give an example on an earthly scale that emphasizes the importance of perfection, the United States government lost $2 million in revenue because of a misplaced comma on the Tariff Act of June 6, 1872. In another example, excluding a single word in the 1631 printing of the Bible promoted rampant promiscuity[1].

The expectation to measure up to God's standards might seem rather far-fetched and even out of reach of human reasoning, but we cannot reenter Heaven in imperfection. Somehow, we must escape normality; we must enter the spiritual realm, though fully human, and continue the lifestyle that Jesus started while He was here on the Earth. This feat is possible with dedication, commitment, Holy Spirit power (not only willpower), and adequate, life-transforming information or insight. I will explain how virtually everyone practices perfection every day, but there is a level of thought and deed that we must aspire to, obtain, and maintain to return home to see the face of God. Our timely and essential duty is to grasp that we can only offer God what He has given us. Why? We are imperfect and produce more imperfections of our own; He is perfect, which is all He can accept. The more obedient we become, the more of His perfection we acquire, and, in turn, the more we can do to please Him. Imperfection is a characteristic of Earth and Hell, not of Heaven. There is no room in His presence or dwelling for anything but perfection. Therefore, we press on to what lies ahead in Christ Jesus:

> *Brothers, I do not consider that I have made it my own. But one thing I do: forgetting what lies behind and straining forward to what lies ahead, I press on toward the goal for the prize of the upward call of God in Christ Jesus. (Philippians 3:13-14, ESV)*

Multiple categorizations of requirements support multiple standards for perfection. If your employer tells you to deliver a package to a certain location and you deposit it according to his or her request, then you have executed the request perfectly.

There are strict prerequisites and standards for living in Heaven. The same is true for Hell. In other words, no one enters Heaven or Hell without being qualified or with a failing grade. Each day of a person's life is a minor or major quiz that accumulates to a final grade. A soul is sent to the appropriate region in the afterlife; the region with which they are compatible. So, in a sense, rejection of God is another form of perfection. It is the perfect or complete acceptance of the deceiver of our souls.

Ordinarily, perfection is not a guaranteed one-time, fixed state of being because our lives are complex, multipart experiences steeped in repetition or recurrences. For instance, the test or temptation you overcame yesterday or a month ago may deliver you a knockout punch in the future, or what has chronically defeated you for years may finally be dealt a fatal blow through vigorous work and commitment to God. Another reason we strive to maintain perfection is opposition: perfection is not a question in Heaven because there is no Devil or opposing being there. Every aspect of Heaven is perfect because Heaven is oneness; every aspect of the Celestial City works and cooperates as a single whole, with no divisions or fragmentation.

As mentioned above, a working definition of perfection is to have something "done thoroughly or completely." That definition, though, might be too broad, particularly for someone who wants to reenter Heaven. Why? In Heaven, there is one standard; on Earth, there are two: God's and humans'. However, our standard is framed by free will. If our standards of thoughts, expectations, and conduct align with God's, then the quality of our decisions will have eternal value. Otherwise, we embody merely imperfection. For example, suppose the same employer whom I introduced above asks an employee to falsify an accounting record. In this case, although the employee knowingly completes the request perfectly and passes the human test, he has failed God's level of perfection.

God is merciful, and His system of justice or divine constitution accounts for ignorance and fairly addresses matters where the wrongdoer has not knowingly, maliciously, or disrespectfully committed an offense. Orientation (toward Heaven or not) or intention of the heart is where God looks for perfection. According to 1 Corinthians 2:11, only God, through His Spirit, knows the heart and objective:

> *For who knows a person's thoughts except his Spirit [or God] within him? In the same way, no one knows the thoughts of God except the Spirit of God.*

In this scenario, a person may perform outwardly perfectly, but the person's soul or heart may fail the perfection test, as we see in Matthew 15:8-9:

> *This people honors Me with their lips, but their heart is far from me. They worship Me in vain, teaching as doctrines human commands.*

Likewise, a person who hates you intensely could, with a smile, give you a gift at your office's Christmas gift exchange party.

> *But Daniel **purposed** [or **intentioned**] in his heart that he would not defile himself with the portion of the king's meat, nor with the wine which he drank."* (Daniel 1:8, KJV)

Though intention is vital when assessing perfection, as is demonstrated in Daniel 1:8 above, consistency is perhaps perfection's hallmark feature. Steadfastness demonstrates a commitment to and sincerity toward doing right and repeating that same level of interest and proficiency until the doer or the standard no longer exist. Occasions for proving consistency arrive like the untiring waves of the sea; some crest higher than those you have seen before, some are of equal height and fierceness, and still, some appear less threatening. All, though, are allowed by God to test your faithfulness to Him, your sincerity in wanting to serve Him, and your fitness to reenter Heaven. To that end, do you know why many might not make it back to Heaven? Because they fail the consistency test. Let us strive to pass that test in Jesus's name.

> *This Jesus is the stone rejected by you builders, which*

> has become the cornerstone. There is salvation in no one else, for there is no other name under heaven given to people by which we must be saved. (Acts 4:11-12, CSB)

Each human is on what is expected to be a relentless quest to be more and more like Jesus, to become Jesus in thoughts and deeds through patience.

> But let patience have its perfect work, that you may be perfect and complete, lacking nothing. (James 1:4, NKJV)

Joyfully entering the road to Heaven and then deciding to depart or to become a prodigal son or daughter is a surefire example of inconsistency. Jesus provides a description in Luke 9:62 of this falling away or backsliding: "But Jesus said to him, no one who puts his hand to the plow and looks back is fit for the kingdom of God." 2 Peter 2:22 provides a similar reference: "It has happened to them according to the true proverb: A dog returns to its own vomit" and "a washed sow returns to wallowing in the mud." To have followed Jesus perfectly, one would have to be consistent to the very end for a lifetime.

Up to this point, we have surveyed God's and humans' standards of perfection. I have illustrated that perfection is, in a very strict sense, the completion of a request according to an established standard or expectation of Earth or Heaven. Nonetheless, we know that we cannot reenter Heaven on human terms. Why? We are imperfect, we are fallen beings, so despite God's great love for us, we cannot offer Him anything in our carnal capacities, and Isaiah 64:6 tells us who we are outside of Christ or in doing anything that He has not approved or ordained:

> *But we are all as an unclean thing, and all our righteousness are as filthy rags; and we all do fade as a leaf, and our iniquities, like the wind, have taken us away.*

> *Blessed are the pure [perfect] in heart: for they shall see God.* (Matthew 5:8, KJV)

With such a firm position on holiness, how then can a human, a fallen, imperfect being, ever get the chance to see the face of God again? To do so we must become **spiritually perfect**, as the subtitle of this chapter informs us. Our perfection is by proxy, with Jesus as the representative or substitute. Jesus is the only standard of perfection that God, His Father, accepts. Anyone trying to ascend the heights of Heaven after death will fail unless they are clothed with the righteousness of Christ.

> **So whoever has God's Son [Christ Jesus] has life;** *whoever does not have his Son, does not have life.* (1 John 5:12, TLB)

Unless we have a relationship with Christ in this life, we have no hope of ever seeing Him again. We certainly will not see His smiling, welcoming face, but rather only Him as a Judge who exercises wrath on all those who rejected Him and opted to remain in imperfection. Our heavenly perfection is in Christ alone, no one else. Performance-related perfection, moral intention, and consistency are undeniably important; indeed, they are so relevant that the Bible warns us in James 2:14-17 that faith without works is dead:

> *What doth it profit, my brethren, though a man say he*

> hath faith, and have not works? can faith save him? If a brother or sister be naked, and destitute of daily food, And one of you say unto them, depart in peace, be ye warmed and filled; notwithstanding ye give them not those things which are needful to the body; what doth it profit? Even so faith, if it hath not works, is dead.

Finally, the following verses describe areas of perfection and imperfection, deeds and misdeeds that impact our potential to reenter Heaven:

> But when the Holy Spirit controls our lives he will produce this kind of fruit in us: **love, joy, peace, patience, kindness, goodness, faithfulness, gentleness and self-control.** (Galatians 5:22-23, TLB)
>
> Be perfect, therefore, as your heavenly Father is perfect. (Matthew 5:48, CSB)

— — AREAS OF PERFECTION

> But when you follow your own wrong inclinations, your lives will produce these evil results: **impure thoughts, eagerness for lustful pleasure, idolatry, spiritism (that is, encouraging the activity of demons), hatred and fighting, jealousy and anger, constant effort to get the best for yourself, complaints and criticisms, the feeling that everyone else is wrong except those in your own little group—and there will be wrong doctrine, envy, murder, drunkenness, wild parties,** and all that sort of thing. Let me tell you again, as I have before, that anyone living that sort of life [that

imperfect life] will not inherit the Kingdom of God. (Galatians 5:19-21, TLB)

— — AREAS OF IMPERFECTION

---

1. Sears, Kathleen. Grammar 101 (Adams 101) (p. 6). Adams Media. Kindle Edition.

I

60+ THINGS TO CONSIDER

HEAVEN IS WATCHING US

The pathway to Heaven is roughly paved with concrete for some miles, relatively as smooth as a runway for several stretches, layered with sharp gravel over perceived never-ending distances, and almost entirely obstructed and impassable at times owing to swift-flowing torrents. However, the road is travelable through Christ Jesus; He has completed the same journey and is now watching and encouraging us as we progress toward Him.

> *Since we have such a huge crowd of men of faith watching us from the grandstands, let us strip off anything that slows us down or holds us back, and especially those sins that wrap themselves so tightly around our feet and trip us up; and let us run with patience the particular race that God has*

set before us. Keep your eyes on Jesus, our leader and instructor. He was willing to die a shameful death on the cross because of the joy he knew would be his afterwards; and now he sits in the place of honor by the throne of God. (Hebrews 12:1-2, TLB)

THE JOURNEY'S CHECKLIST
KEEP YOUR HEART WITH ALL DILIGENCE

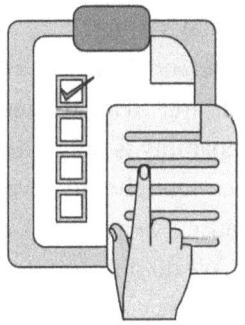

*T*he following is a checklist of quick and timely ponderable points covering a wide variety of spiritual matters.

GOD IN ALL AND THROUGH ALL

1. Each person's life is an animated expression of God's thoughts and will.

2. Each life is more important to God than every single earthly thing that is taking place right now. We have countless reasons to smile.
3. If God is not in control, then someone else is. Can you imagine the alternative?
4. We are from Heaven because our Creator is from there. We are born with infinite power but can end up going nowhere. Living and dying without Christ is to head nowhere or to go to a place that is utterly unknown called Hell. The Bible informs us that God, by His Spirit of limitless strength, lives in and through everything. He lives in us, thereby enabling us to do His will, to do whatever He allows. Therefore, we are accountable for allocating and managing the energy or life that His Spirit provides. Why use His power to end up in the enemy's camp?
5. All skills are from God. Whether a person is a programmer, plumber, dentist, racecar driver, or teacher, their capability is only a drop from an infinite pool of resources. One should never handle a talent with pride, because it belongs to God. We only possess the gift. We do not own it.
6. When God speaks, He commands, and His words are asphalt that form the narrow road back to Heaven. The Bible is a book of God's unchangeable instructions. The term "command" implies a certain level of strictness and straightness. For example, the familiar cliché, "straight as an arrow", portrays an accurate image of an absolute command to follow a fixed path.
7. What does it mean that we can do nothing without Christ? Everything requires life or energy, and God Himself is life. Therefore, whether the action is good or evil, it is done with His strength. However, those

who use His life to do wrong have used God's investment of power as an accomplice in an offense. Forgiveness and repentance are therefore required to remedy the fallout to avoid eternal separation from Him.

8. Anyone who is a Christian and has claimed to never witness a miracle perhaps needs to engage in a closer self-inspection. What is a miracle? It is an improbable event. For example, the process of salvation is a supernatural undertaking that transforms a soul from darkness to light, from the griminess and disease-ridden spiritual being of sin to a condition that is acceptable in His sight.

9. During life's challenges, one might reason that God is nowhere to be found, but Hebrews 13:5 reminds us that He "will never leave you nor forsake you." How can we be sure that He is with us? We know this because each person has three members: body, soul, and Spirit. Since <u>the Spirit is the life in each person</u>, it is more than reasonable to conclude that He is with you because you are reading this—you are alive.

GOD GAVE ME TODAY, NOT TOMORROW

1. Today, think about the number of seconds you are spending on engagements that do not increase your precious eternal worth and then consider that everyone beneath your feet this moment is begging to be in your place for just one second. Every lost soul was arguably busy with plans for a better future. Sadly, they decidedly placed more emphasis on distractions.

2. Nearly everyone has a romanticized or idealized

understanding that everything belongs to God and that He is in control, but do we live what we confess? If I were to tell you that your life is not your own and that it belongs to God, would you practically believe? One day I began to take a deep dive into that question, and I realized that if my answer is yes, then why do we worry and fret? Why do we wrestle God for our will? Why do we steam inside when things appear contrary to a plan or an expectation? Why? Perhaps we want to seize the helm from Him and side with the impoliteness of impatience and feed the ravenous appetite for control. I don't know about you, but I find it remarkably challenging and sometimes suffocating to live a life admittedly that is not mine or to have God live through me, using and controlling the space allocated to me called free will. We become perfect at godly living by mastering the process of dying to self-will. Until our souls actively "let go and let God," Hell will continue to enlarge itself with much pomp, as Isaiah 5:14 reminds us: "Therefore Hell hath enlarged herself and opened her mouth without measure, and their glory, and their multitude, and their pomp, and he that rejoiceth, shall descend into it."

3. Unless the intention is to find areas for improvement in human interaction, drawing a comparison between oneself and another is ordinarily pointless. It can be destructive because the result usually thumps the comparer into downheartedness and unthankfulness. Those emotions are generally unproductive and displeasing to God. We have to be careful about comparing fallen beings because the effort is similar, if not identical, to measuring false and false or imperfection and imperfection. Yes, we can learn

from others, but Jesus wants us to measure up to Him, the only good and perfect person. Read the Bible to learn about Him, and use it as your guide. The reason for coming to Earth or leaving it has no bearing on another human, only on our Creator. Why waste time with what does not matter anyway—if a person sees you as gold, but you don't have a relationship with Jesus, then where will your eternal residence be when you and your friend are gone from here? Let's think strategically about this life and time; we own none.

4. Perhaps not all, but a countless number of the many souls in Hell today worked on a project or tried to fix an issue before death permanently interrupted their progress. In many cases, their work continued and reached completion.
5. Too often, throughout the world, desires of the flesh tirelessly wrestle to keep one so busy with futility that God gets no time. Eventually, Hell gains another soul, owing to ineffective time management. Today, start fighting against becoming another victim. Remain sober and ever watchful!
6. Considering that God created us in His image, disobedience is a condition that prohibits Him from working in or through His likenesses (human beings). If the situation does not change, He will pursue a willing and obedient person and allow the unwilling soul to follow self-will, resulting in curses, not blessings.
7. Do not ever become lost in the crowd of humanity, the hustle and bustle of life and time. Perhaps the most challenging and critical aspect of life on Earth is maintaining the balance of profitable engagements with other mortals in conjunction with attending to our individualized requirements for reentering

Heaven. We are social beings, but Heaven-sent, mission-specified ones first. Do not lose focus on your accountability to God. Doing so will be eternally disastrous. No one can help you but Him—never forget this point. The apparent never-ending togetherness we share with others ends at death, where new interactions begin.

8. Who wants to become eternal garbage? When a soul leaves Heaven, it is a perfectly fitting component, working flawlessly in that celestial system. While on the Earth, owing to the wear and tear of the destructive process known as sin, that soul becomes malformed, even developing sharp and jagged edges. If timely corrections are not made through repentance, the soul becomes misshapen and incompatible when death ships it back to the door of Heaven, where it will be rejected. The only alternative is the junkyard of the underworld.

9. A familiar question in the Christian world is, "Are you saved?" If the response is "yes", I hope the questioner and the questionee don't leave the conversation thinking that nothing more needs to be done. I believe the answer should not be simply "yes" but "yes, I am being saved daily" to indicate the continuous effort of God in one's life. Christians are being rescued and steadied daily against the gravitational pull of sin—the "yes" answer is best presented in Heaven, not on Earth. Therefore, "Once Saved, Always Saved" (OSAS) is nonsense because we are fallen beings, ever needing the nurturing of God until our final breath.

10. We have to make prayer a profession and strive to become professionals at doing it. Generally, we pray for two reasons: to petition for assistance and give

thanks through praise. Therefore, the instruction in 1 Thessalonians 5:17, "*pray without ceasing*", is an urgent call to praise God and plead for assistance. God included that verse for a reason. When we don't pray or praise, can you imagine the magnitude and impact of the neglect? Neglectfulness is the primary reason why many souls fail to reenter Heaven.

11. Despite how physically healthy and wealthy you are at this moment, if you are not praying to God, the Father of Jesus, you are dying and possibly on your way to eternal destruction. Pause for a moment, and examine your life. The Bible informs us that we can do nothing without God and that we must pray ceaselessly. Why? Because no one is capable of living without Him. The same Bible also says, "*There is a way that seems right to a man, but its end is the way of death.*" (Proverbs 14:12). Can you imagine the millions of lost souls in the same position you are in today? Humans are almost identical, varying primarily by lifestyle choices.

12. Many think the world is quite advanced and that we have made tremendous progress, but compared to what? How does a fallen being measure progress? Can it be determined by the improvements of its inventions or perhaps how close it has risen to the height of its former glory? If we had no soul and were composed only of things entirely from the Earth, then comparing how we are now to how we were then would be logical, even reasonable. In that scenario, the distinction between a horse-drawn carriage and a car would warrant ceaseless praises. However, we are from eternity in the past and will continue into eternity in the future. Life on Earth is nothing more than a blur, perhaps a single day's event in God's eyes.

The Bible compares life to the morning bloom of a flower that withers by the evening. Without question, God wants us to be inventors and innovators and to applaud success. However, during this applause, He wants us to entertain and answer this question: What have you done for your soul to merit an equal cheer? Have you done anything to lift yourself from your fallen condition?

13. Full employment is a goal of any economy and that does not exclude Heaven and Hell. God expects efficiency and effectiveness from His children. Similarly, demons are very skilled fallen beings working tirelessly to destroy souls. Sinning keeps demons busy, even fully employed, with dragging targeted souls to the underworld.
14. Getting back to Heaven requires us to follow a disciplined lifestyle that routinely obeys God. A routine is an invariable strategy for having an expected outcome.

EXPECTATION MANAGEMENT

1. For we all stumble in many things. If anyone does not stumble in word, he is a perfect man, able also to bridle [control] the whole body. (James 3:2, NKJV)
2. Today, undoubtedly, millions are wailing, fretting, and hating under the seemingly unendurable and intense weight of poverty and social unrest, spiritually as well. In such a condition, hardly anyone would want to hear about God's goodness, much less Heaven and far less anything concerning Hell, especially when they consider themselves to be living what is already a hellish life. How can one be

comforted or accept the notion of hope when, in their minds, the world has moved on and left them in the dust? The answer to these questions is *expectation management*. For instance, if you knew that a lion was on the prowl and is potentially crouching in the thicket near your camp, you would prepare for a potential attack. If you did not know of the lurking danger, you may gingerly walk to your lodging and narrowly escape an attack owing to the watchful eyes of a professional hunter, but you would still be mightily upset. When we understand and appreciate that we don't own ourselves, we realize that God owes us nothing, which actually makes us more relaxed and thankful. He ordains or allows everything for our good according to His plan. Fretting is an act of pride that challenges His decision-making, and it is sinful.
3. If your eyes are on yourself or something else, maybe a test or temptation, they are no longer on Jesus. Peter made the same mistake before he began sinking.
4. On Earth, prayer is a priceless privilege because it holds no value in Hell. Yes, stop and think about the many who are praying in the intense inferno at this very moment. Enjoy your present comforts as you pray and praise, because this window of opportunity will eventually close. Everything outside of Christ is a total unrecoverable loss, an unimaginable waste of life, time, and resources. Invest wisely because the eternal investor expects a return on His investment in you, and He is watching and waiting.
5. It is relatively common to hear comments like these: "that a Christian is behaving worse than an unsaved person" or "Buddhists are often more serious or pious about their religion than Christians." Well, Hindus, Muslims, and Jehovah's Witnesses, among others,

tend to be like that because they are not following Christ. They are heading in the same direction and are not meeting the satanic resistance that the hordes of Hell level against those who are faithful to Jesus. Generally, it is conceivable for rivers that merge and flow in the same direction to be smooth and waveless.

6. The Lord sees everything. He watches every good and evil deed under the sun. Prayer is an invitational plea for His involvement in our lives. Without a petition, we are requesting that He maintain distance from us and respect our power to choose.
7. Isaiah 9:6 describes Jesus as the Wonderful Counselor, Mighty God, Everlasting Father, and Prince of Peace. I have proven the peace God's presence gives to a troubled mind, a condition where uncertainty and doubt overwhelming abound. One day, I was precisely in that state of being. I decided to spend about 1–2 hours in quiet before Him. At some point, I did nod off, but all in all, I emerged feeling peaceful. The heaviness had lifted. Try it! I have found that reading the Bible aloud for more than a brief moment, perhaps 30 minutes, has a similar effect.
8. I believe the most effective strategy to combat feelings of hopelessness, worthlessness, and possibly suicide is knowledge. God says my people are destroyed for lack of knowledge. Sometimes the life-saving information is not directly yes or no, but it is about knowing limits. For example, a child's nagging request to visit a candy store may be a definite no. However, the youngster may insist and begin to protest with an irritating bawl. If the headstrong youth truly understands that the effort is useless, the parent would see a change. When limits or boundaries are in place, attitudes or responses follow

suit. Isaiah 26:9 is an example of a limit: *"For when Your judgments are in the Earth, the inhabitants of the world will learn righteousness."* Jesus is God, and God is Jesus, but each has a slightly different role. Jesus is the one who affords us the yes and no options for a lifetime through the opportunity of free will, but it is critical to know and adhere to the limit to reentering Heaven set by His Father, which is holiness. Appropriately, as examples of limits, realizing that it is idolatrous to focus on an issue more than we focus on God is life-saving. Knowing that He only answers the petition offered in faith helps us not to doubt. Understanding that repetition is required to digest His promises easily compels us to read and study verses more than once. Embracing the truth that God cannot change should cause us to scamper from lies, and understanding that no one gets out of the volcanic torments in Hell should cause a mass exodus from unrepentance.

9. From the Bible, we learned that Jesus is God and vice versa. In John 14:8, the disciple Philip said to Jesus, "*Lord, show us the Father,*" and He responded this way in the following verse: "*Have I been with you so long, and yet you have not known Me, Philip? He who has seen Me has seen the Father.*" Therefore, I can accurately write that God, through the person of Jesus, came on the Earth, lived among us, and then died by us for us. God knows everything about suffering and pain in the body and soul; He engineered the process. However, mere mortals do not and cannot share the same understanding of the physical body as Him. For example, a lion can kill the body with a tactical bite accompanied by suffocation, magma from a volcano can reduce it to ashes, and cancer can systematically

diminish it to a skeleton cell by cell. These three methods of destroying the body ensure indescribable pain and terror. However, since there is no fear in God, as perfect love casts it out, nothing moves Him. Yes, He empathizes with those in agony, but it is all a process to achieve a better end if we are willing to work with Him. As such, we dare not think that our loving God, using divine justice, won't allow sin to subject the disobedient and unrepentant to the crucible of unquenched fire in Hell—that, too, is a process, except to no value for the lost.

10. Today, each time you eat, please consider your soul. It, too, has needs. God will hold us responsible for neglecting our souls. Many people end up in Hell for poor stewardship. Pursuing a sinful lifestyle is the fastest way to destroy one's soul. Not reading the Bible and avoiding prayer are equally irresponsible ways of neglecting God's investment of life and time in us. Remember, we have two kids to feed, not just the one that cries the loudest and is physically accessible in the visible world. The unseen one is more important.

11. Whenever you feel all hope is gone, that no one loves you or even cares, please adjust your mind and bring yourself back from the brink of potential ruin with this truth: the most important and helpful person appreciates you with a perfect love that cannot change. Rest in that reality and faithful hope. He cannot lie.

12. Without a doubt, we cannot get back to Heaven using mortal capabilities, as the Celestial City, a spiritual world, does not conduct business with mere humans. Therefore, we have to form an alliance or partnership, as it were, with someone. The Spirit of God is that

person. We must strictly comply with Him and make no exceptions. He alone enables all interactions and conversions from darkness to light and mortality to immortality. The "7 Steps Homeward" explains how to work with Him.
13. Praise the Lord if you are punished for doing right! Of course, you get no credit for being patient if you are beaten for doing wrong; but if you do right and suffer for it, and are patient beneath the blows, God is well pleased. This suffering is all part of the work God has given you. Christ, who suffered for you, is your example. Follow in his steps: He never sinned, never told a lie, never answered back when insulted; when he suffered he did not threaten to get even; he left his case in the hands of God who always judges fairly. (1 Peter 2:19-23, TLB)

CONSIDERING OTHERS

1. The Lord is constantly seeking ways to bless us. For example, when He said it is more blessed to give than to receive, it was to fulfill promises found in verses like Luke 6:381: "*Give, and it shall be given unto you; good measure, pressed down, and shaken together, and running over, shall men give into your bosom. For with the same measure that ye mete withal it shall be measured to you again.*" We are technically and legally excluded from the declaration of that verse when we don't share. Therefore, use every opportunity to give a helping hand.
2. Why are gossiping and backbiting obstructive, alienating behaviors? Such misconduct pits images of God against themselves. A human being is the

representative or image of God veiled in the flesh for a lifetime.

3. Why do some people lie and cheat? I believe the answer is the unwillingness to be truthful to oneself and others and to face the fact of being a mere human. Bernie Madoff, notorious for swindling billions from investors, was an ambitious guy from Queens, New York, who grew up in a middle-class family. He opened his trading company in 1960 with a small roster of investors, but the stock market rocked a bit in 1962, and he lost about $3,000. Instead of owning up the risk of doing business by telling clients of their losses, embarrassment led him to mask the failure; he borrowed the money from his father-in-law. That was a disastrous decision because it would lead him to the profession of lying that eventually costs clients upwards of 65 billion in fraudulent losses. He ended up in prison and died there.

> *Speak evil of no man, to be no brawlers, but gentle, shewing all meekness unto all men. For we ourselves also were sometimes foolish, disobedient, deceived, serving divers lusts and pleasures, living in malice and envy, hateful, and hating one another. (Titus 3:2-3, KJV)*

FORGIVENESS & SALVATION

1. At His crucifixion, Jesus prayed to His Father to forgive His accusers and crucifiers. The statement "forgive them for they knew not what they had done" should include "to Jesus." Personalizing the expression

to such a degree highlights that they did not know Jesus because no one can honestly know Him. Romans 11:33 teaches that He is unsearchable, and John 3:8 describes Him as the wind. Thank God for the opportunity of forgiveness.

2. Why is it so important to speedily seek forgiveness and repentance? Living in an unrepentant state is like trying to fight an enemy with holes in one's shield. The longer one takes to repair the breach by putting off seeking forgiveness and pursuing repentance, the more time and impact the enemy has to establish a foothold.

3. If you ever doubt God's plan of salvation for you and the entire world, I have a corrective message to share. In the Old Testament, specifically in Exodus 13:17, there is a most vital nugget of insight: "Then it came to pass when Pharaoh had let the people go, that God did not lead them by way of the land of the Philistines, although that was near; for God said, lest perhaps the people change their minds when they see war and return to Egypt." Of the number of lessons one can glean from that pivotal verse, I will tell you of the two presently accessible to my understanding. First, the Lord demonstrated compassion by using a strategy to avoid conflict with the Philistines, considering they had just left years of suffering in slavery. Indeed, there were those amongst them capable of fierce defense, but the majority, I reason, would have been decimated. Second, the Lord always wants to teach the emotional virtues of patience and spiritual stamina. Instead of allowing the relatively quick advance through the land of the Philistines and using angelic support to overwhelm the enemy, God decided to take them through the wilderness toward

the Red Sea. Living on Earth is synonymous with the Red Sea experience; we have to cross it.
4. If you ever doubt God's love for you, probably owing to an emotional sway or deceit, then accept His love logically. If He does not love you, then He loves no one because He is the totality of love. Love is more than a characteristic of His. It is Who He is. Moreover, if He could decrease in love, even in the slightest way, He would become Satan's friend, sharing an evil attribute and we would no longer have a righteous God. Trust the authenticity of His perfect love. We can go to Him unafraid or unbowed. He is always waiting for us without a hint of condemnation. "There is therefore now no condemnation to those who are in Christ Jesus, who do not walk according to the flesh, but according to the Spirit," Romans 8:1.
5. Come, let's talk this over, says the Lord; no matter how deep the stain of your sins, I can take it out and make you as clean as freshly fallen snow. Even if you are stained as red as crimson, I can make you white as wool! If you will only let me help you, if you will only obey, then I will make you rich! But if you keep on turning your backs and refusing to listen to me, you will be killed by your enemies; I, the Lord, have spoken. (Isaiah 1:18-20, TLB)
6. According to *Theopedia.com*, "The Age of Accountability is that time in the development of a person when he or she can and invariably does sin against God and thus stands in the need of personal redemption through Jesus Christ." It is an accurate definition, but, of course, God alone knows that day or moment. A trespasser might not know that an act is an offense, so daily repentance for known and

unknown sins is required. Though a child may brush away its first sinful thought or deed owing to ignorance, matters might have been quite different for Adam and Eve, who were practically adults but possibly still spiritually young. Their transition from innocence to accountability is recorded in Genesis 3:6 when they ate the forbidden fruit. Up to and until that moment, they were in a heavenly place, but disobedience oversaw their departure. Likewise, when we live clean, repentant lives, we enter paradise, the home of God, lost to the first couple. However, we suffer the same fate as the initial Adamic family when we pursue sinfulness: expulsion from heavenly accommodations until repentance.

UNEXPECTED LESSONS

1. James 5:16 informs that "the effectual fervent prayer of a righteous man availeth much." In other words, the earnest prayer of a righteous man has great power and excellent results. Why? There is something special about praying for someone whose shoes you have not only stepped into but also have made some strides in. When you are familiar with a condition, especially a painful or distressing one, your intercession will have more passion and compassion. We don't always have to learn by going into the desert. In my experience, particularly since no one has time and resources to experience and endure all the rigors of life, obedience is the better teacher of lessons that disobedience teaches the hard way. As your soul passes each obedience test, it immediately benefits from the decision; it does not have to wait to

potentially acquire value as it suffers through hardship over an unintended, possibly lengthy period. Obedience is efficient learning, which is God's preferred approach to teaching His children.

2. Acts 2:4 provides evidence of the disciples speaking in a non-native language: "And they were all filled with the Holy Spirit and began to speak with other tongues, as the Spirit gave them utterance." In James 1:19, we are encouraged (or warned) to be swift listeners but slow speakers: "So then, my beloved brethren, let every man be swift to hear, slow to speak, slow to wrath." Speaking in tongues is a conversation with God through the Holy Spirit in a language that not even Satan understands: "For the person who speaks in another tongue is not speaking to people but to God, since no one understands him; he speaks mysteries in the Spirit," 1 Corinthians 14:2. In today's technological world, that interaction is called secure communication. I believe being slow to speak offers a small fraction of the benefits of speaking in tongues because, though Satan can learn tendencies, he does not have access to the content of our minds. However, he can predict our behavior using our history of sins. Therefore, monitor what you say because invisible agents are listening. What you say can be used against you.

3. In James 4:12, we read that "There is one Lawgiver, who is able to save and to destroy. Who are you to judge another?" Luke 6:37 offers a similar warning: "Judge not, and you shall not be judged. Condemn not, and you shall not be condemned. Forgive, and you will be forgiven." Why is our Lord giving us these strict instructions? Identical to the function of the other restrictions and commands pasted across

the Bible pages, the aim is to keep us from self-destruction. However, it is difficult, even impossible, for us to judge one another to a level pleasing to God. Judging others is assuming the role of God or acting as one who is perfect. Such an attempt impersonates Him and exposes the one casting judgment as a potential liar who claims to have complete information about the matter or person. Indeed, full information is in the soul and is not necessarily what is expressed vocally or through body language. Only God knows all the hidden aspects of thought or deed. We have three parts (body, soul, and Spirit), and often we only see what the body conveys, which accounts for barely one-third of a human being.

4. Never underestimate your worth. Today, are you a manager? Do you ever doubt how far-reaching your decisions are? You might ask yourself, "If God is good all the time, then why are multitudes doomed to eternal ruin"? Yes, God is unendingly good, but your management input can save you from joining those multitudes in endless regrets. You might not be a CEO or a department manager, but God has appointed you as an executive of an asset more important than the physical Earth and all its operations: it is your life, your eternity. Why is your life unimaginably valuable? It equals the life of Christ; He did not die for anything less than an image of Himself. Our decisions are so personally all-embracing and eternally weighty that uninterrupted joy or pain is the reward. Many don't reenter Heaven because they don't understand their role or its significance. Instead, they neglect or abandon stewardship, resting on the lofty, misleading idea that

because God is good all the time, all is well with their souls.

5. Body language is nonverbal communication. However, it is no different from spoken language in the eyes of God because they have the same source: His image or the soul. Therefore, expressions of bitterness, resentment, spitefulness, murmur, complaint, rudeness, and profanity are equally as sinful as a disrespectful eye-roll, frown, clenched fist, lip biting, hands on hips, and rapid finger-tapping. Yes, our bodies are the temples of God, and in this physical world, they showcase God in us if we allow it. Let's try to put forth a good impression—we are His image.

6. Do you believe that love does not harm? Do you understand that love defends its own? John 3:16 declares, "*For God so loved the world that He gave His only begotten Son, that whoever believes in Him should not perish but have everlasting life.*" Do you accept the declaration in John 3:16? If you answer yes to all three questions, stop, think, and realize that you do not need to complain, murmur, fret, or hate. Perhaps unknowingly, we reject His love and sacrifice when we engage in any such misconduct and hinder Him from helping us. Rest in the assurance that God is working everything for your good. He did not die for us just because He had nothing else to do. Sin reduces the soul to such a deplorable condition that only His death could have redeemed or rescue it. His life is His investment in us, and that tells of our importance. There is hope after all. Rejoice! Choose to give thanks, not unthankfulness, less you hurt yourself.

7. If God intended for you to live on Earth in endless happiness but denied you the privilege and allowed

the opposite, then He won't be the God who is perfect in love; He would be bad-minded, and the world would have more issues than we can imagine. Don't you agree? Of course, our loving Creator can never be bad-minded; that's the work of Satan and demons. Now, if we believe that God is 100% efficient and effective and He controls everything, why do we protest in anger and murmur against any displeasure? Are we more productive than him? Yes, God is sympathetic to our needs. However, and perhaps astonishingly so, the truth is that He is less concerned about our earthly pleasures and entirely more about our eternal worth. Why? Everything is passing away. He cannot use any in Heaven, and neither can you in your eternal home.

8. Envy is a silent protest or disapproval of what God is doing in someone else's life. Thereby making this behavior a malicious, trespassing act.
9. Day by day, life is an essay each person composes moment by moment, but it is never error-free due to the writer's imperfections. Jesus is the only editor who can turn one's writing into a composition acceptable to God, the assignment giver.
10. Whether it is tangible or intangible, everything that enters someone's life is ordained or allowed by God to test or tempt the soul to draw it closer heavenward.
11. The human body is a stage where the soul performs before Heaven and Hell at the courtesy and privilege of God's grace and free will.
12. Salvation is a beautification process that revives and transforms a soul from darkness to light, from a sin-based, disease-infested existence to a being that is precious and acceptable in God's sight.
13. We often associate a testimony to a miraculous

increase in health, finance, or otherwise. Therefore, it is not uncommon for someone to smilingly stand before a small group or large congregation narrating God's blessings. However, not all testimonies leave the audience smiling; some provoke quick and strict reverential fear. In Acts 5, Ananias and Sapphira's lies testify that God could use any circumstance to keep His children on the narrow path. The husband-and-wife duo had sold a possession but lied about the price to keep back a portion. This transgression resulted in their deaths, and the frightful and instructive testimony that followed caused great fear upon all the church. Every outcome is a testimony, but pride encourages us to hide many. Nonetheless, we only have to recognize the value in each one and give thanks in everything.

14. Perhaps some are unaware that the Bible is not a book for God; it is a way for humans to find Him. He does not need it. Why? Perfection does not require support; only imperfection does.

15. Some time ago, I watched a video in which a person was describing her experience in Heaven. The event occurred one night after she had fallen asleep while wrestling with a troubling, undiagnosed illness. From her vantage point in Heaven, she had the opportunity to observe her body at rest in her bed while having a conversation with an angel. The angel told the woman that she had died and her current body is eternal. She asked the celestial being, and I paraphrase, "How could I be dead when I am here talking with you?" God's messenger responded in a manner equivalent to this: "Whenever someone goes to sleep, that person is practically dead unless the Lord decides to wake him or her." Cleary, tomorrow

is not promised. It is a gift. The sobering and hopefully gripping truth is that today is what God has given us. Tomorrow is merely a prospect, not a promise. Eternity is just a single breath away. Now, do you have any concerns or rejections about why we should live in constant preparedness to arrive before Him? Praying every morning and evening, and even in between, is a wise and productive effort to remain fit for Heaven. Don't forget to read the Bible and practice kindness.

16. Death is the destruction of the body, but it does not destroy our true self (the soul). This process is merely the uncoupling or splitting of the "human being" into two distinct members: human and being. The process can also be seen as the separation of the finite from the infinite.

17. To effectively believe in Jesus, one has to do His will by abiding in Him through consistent obedience, not just saying: "I love Jesus" or "I believe in Him." Talk and thoughts are cheap. The life of Christ is expensive, but offered freely until our life ends on Earth. Make wise use of your moment of grace.

18. Let no man say when he is tempted, I am tempted of God: for God cannot be tempted with evil, neither tempteth he any man: But every man is tempted, when he is drawn away of his own lust, and enticed. (James 1:13-14, KJV)

19. These six things doth the LORD hate: yea, seven are an abomination unto him: A proud look, a lying tongue, and hands that shed innocent blood, a heart that deviseth wicked imaginations, feet that be swift in running to mischief, a false witness that speaketh lies, and he that soweth discord among brethren. (Proverbs 6:16-19, KJV)

II

7 STEPS HOMEWARD

A GUIDE TO SURVIVING LIFE ON EARTH

A man's heart plans his way, but the Lord directs his steps. (Proverbs 16:9, NKJV)

The intention of the "7 Steps Homeward" is to introduce a convenient strategy for developing the kind of lifestyle that demonstrate a commitment to holiness. As such, these steps are less a strict order of operations than an adaptable, yet clearly outlined, lifestyle change. (The exceptions are Steps 1 and 2, crucial for starting and maintaining a relationship with God through Christ.) They address forgiveness and repentance. We always seek forgiveness first and demonstrate responsibility for and commitment to repentance. The remaining five (pray and fast, worship, serve, study, and sanctify) equally important steps are mission-critical practices for maintaining the first two and can be done in any order.

Trust in the Lord with all thine heart, and lean not unto thine own understanding. In all thy ways acknowledge Him, and He shall direct thy paths. (Proverbs 3:5-6, KJV)

For I know the thoughts that I think toward you, saith the Lord, thoughts of peace, and not of evil, to give you an expected end. (Jeremiah 29:11, KJV)

Who is a God like You, who pardons wrongdoing And passes over a rebellious act of the remnant of His possession? ***He does not retain His anger forever, because He delights in mercy.*** *(Micah 7:18, NASB)*

O my people, what have I [your God] done that makes you turn away from me? *Tell me why your patience is exhausted! Answer me! (Micah 6:3, TLB)*

Mankind, He has told each of you what is good and what it is the LORD requires of you: ***to act justly, to love faithfulness, and to walk humbly with your God.*** *(Micah 6:8, CSB)*

*[**Because of sin,**]* ***You will sow but not reap;*** *you will press olives but not anoint yourself with oil, and you will tread grapes but not drink the wine. (Micah 6:15, CSB)*

Jesus accepted the total weight of sin to sponsor our return to Heaven. This is also why He took upon Himself the flesh or the physical nature of humans. Christ is God, and God cannot die! Therefore, to die for our sins, He had to become human through Jesus. "Who, being in the form of God, thought it not robbery to be equal with God: But made himself of no reputation, and took upon him the form of a servant, and was made in the likeness of men: And being found in fashion as a man, he humbled himself, and became obedient unto death, even the death of the cross." (Philippians 2:6-8, KJV)

INTRODUCTION

Going back to Heaven is a personal, eventful, freewill-based decision; you must be ready to climb.

A man's heart plans his way, but the Lord directs his steps. (Proverbs 16:9 NKJV)

*T*hought-provoking and sobering questions challenge our thinking patterns daily. Why do people kill each other? Why do we hate and feel bitterness? Why do many people step on and over each other when they will eventually stand before the same holy God or be doomed forever with the prince of fallen angels? Why do we torpedo each other with foul responses, cut down each other with backbiting and gossip, spend far too many days chasing the proverbial wind, and seek the pleasures of tomorrow while avoiding the preparations that are required today? Why don't we think and plan for the future beyond securing food for the stomach and enough money to buy more food? Why do we always want Heaven on Earth when it is not possible? Why do we protest or murmur when asked to do things that are God's will? Why do we live as if we will never die? Why do we look for Jesus in the sky and ignore Him in another human being? Why? Why? Why?

Questions like these cannot be ignored. I believe we sometimes develop spiritual myopia. I don't think we appreciate that we are not exactly what we see in the mirror. We are intrinsically the same, differing only by the unique bundle of life's decisions. That's all. Can you think of any other differences that do not fade away in the grave?

Deciding to follow Christ is our only option to escape eternal suffering. Earth is like a preview of Heaven and Hell. It is a lifelong window-shopping experience. Every event, whether successful or unsuccessful, whether it brings pain, joy, laughter, or sadness, presents us with a follow-up question: "Do you want more of this?" Hell is the source of hatefulness, while Heaven is the realm of loving-kindness. Pray and choose what you want more of wisely.

In this section, "7 Strategies for Reentering Heaven," you will find guidelines for how to remedy failings in human interactions and how to interface with our heavenly Father for vital support as we prepare for the journey back to Heaven. As you move through each step, be aware that the tests and temptations in your life are not idle chances. You may be surprised to realize they represent the amount of work God and His angels are doing to prepare you for reentering Heaven. At times it may be painful, as they scrub the grime of sin away from the soul. We often label such challenges as judgments, punishments, or God being harsh, which is a disrespectful view. He does not do or allow anything without a purpose, and fighting his purpose in our lives is sinful.

The choice of seven steps is purposeful because that number holds significance in Christendom; it represents completion. For instance, God took six days to create the Earth and rested on the seventh. There are other examples such as these from the book of Revelation:

- Seven churches (1:4)
- Seven golden lamp stands (1:12)
- Seven stars (1:16)
- Seven seals (5:1)
- Seven trumpets (8:6)

Do not consider the prescribed steps as a rigid progression, like rungs on a ladder that sequentially lead to the top. Instead, weigh and apply them as methods to manage specific errors, individual slips, rather than a comprehensive plan for your entire life. Doing so will keep you from becoming overwhelmed. For example, if you backbite, try applying this prescription:

1. Tell Jesus you are sorry (ask forgiveness).
2. Control the tendency to avoid a recurrence (repent).
3. Petition for strength and wisdom to prevent recurrences (pray).
4. Acknowledge, with thanksgiving, you can do all things through Christ who strengthens you (worship).
5. Focus on the good in the person and pray for them to overcome the challenge, if applicable (serve).

6. Read what the Bible says about the topic of backbiting (study).
7. Try to maintain those six steps (sanctify).

If you slide from rung 6 to 3 and then rise from 3 to 4, keep trying. The goal is to arrive at seven and stay there for that issue and all the others.

Many years ago, I watched an advertisement that showcased how accurately a bank processes its checks. They described their challenge, saying it's not about the millions of checks they process, but processing each check correctly and repeating that step millions of times.

The goal is to handle each sin, each wrongdoing, with the steps needed to remain spiritually healthy. That's the process of becoming perfect—addressing each violation completely and correctly. Fortunately, the expectation here is not as extensive as the Talmud, the full gamut of Jewish law and tradition compiled into 613 commandments (mitzvot) in the Torah. There are only seven steps here, which can serve as a starting point for your development. We must endure suffering and difficulties, stay focused on the journey, and strive until we reach the end.

> And **if the righteous scarcely be saved, where shall the ungodly and the sinner appear?** Wherefore let them that suffer according to the will of God commit the keeping of their souls to Him in well doing, as unto a faithful Creator. (1 Peter 4:18-19, KJV)

Lao Tzu, the Chinese philosopher, coined the now-famous quote, "The journey of a thousand miles begins with one step." The spokesperson and civil rights leader Martin Luther King Jr. said, "If you can't fly then run, if you can't run then walk, if you can't walk then crawl, but whatever you do you must keep moving forward."

These quotes are essentially rephrasing of Jesus' teaching about the challenge of passing through the narrow gate. He tells us that we must strive with resolute intention and sincere effort to enter Heaven. No one gets back home by mortal tenacity alone; though Jesus will help us, we still must fight the good fight to overcome sin. Otherwise, our transgressions will barricade the narrow pathway, forever separating us from our native home unless the bulldozer of repentance removes the blockade.

> ***Strive to enter in at the strait gate***, *for many, I say unto you, will seek to enter in, and shall not be able. (Luke 13:24, KJV)*

> ***Enter ye in at the strait gate, for wide is the gate, and broad is the way, that leads to destruction,*** *and many there be which go in thereat. Because strait is the gate, and narrow is the way, which leads unto life, and few there be that find it. (Matthew 7:13-14, KJV)*

> ***Fight the good fight of faith***, *lay hold on eternal life, whereunto thou art also called, and hast professed a good profession before many witnesses. (1 Timothy 6:12, KJV)*

Sinning is a very advanced and deceptive operation that is often perpetrated by demons. It deceives because its consequences are often not realized immediately, which may give the trespasser the false impression that all is well. Further, we are only children, created lower than angels, even the fallen ones. As a result, we are outmatched against dark forces, far out of our league. We need help! We need Jesus. But we do not need to fear because God is alive. He wants to help us find the narrow path and to remain on it, homeward bound.

> *Fear not, for I am with you; be not dismayed, for I am your God. I will strengthen you, Yes, I will help you,* I will uphold you with My righteous right hand. (Isaiah 41:10, NKJV)

Living on Earth is not a cakewalk; it's a trek over peaks and through valleys. There are sinister beings from antiquity who are specialists at destroying humans. A counterstrategy is required to stem the tide of destruction, but merely wanting to live a holy life isn't enough at this point. This section will provide a template to help guide your efforts to sustain your spiritual growth. The biblically-based "7 Steps Homeward" checklist is a model and assessment tool I use personally and in evangelistic sessions to cover what is required to stay focused on the mission of reentering Heaven. We should use these steps and strategies to stave off the buildup of sins on our souls.

Consider that the world is a system of operations put into effect before the first human was created. This system does not change. For example, wrong and right were determined when God wrote the divine rulebook. Since we cannot modify the standards, wisdom encourages us to learn about them to avoid breaking the rules. Jesus knows we will make mistakes along the way, but He never wants us to feel condemned. He did not come to criticize anyone. We only must accept His mercy and turn from any wrongdoing. In other words, there is no need to feel so guilty or ashamed that you think He would no longer want to hear from you. Restoring us to joy and peace is His specialty and delight. Please do not allow the enemy to make you think differently because that approach only steers you off the narrow way and blocks you from making it back home.

There is therefore now no condemnation to them which are in Christ Jesus, *who walk not after the flesh, but after the Spirit. (Romans 8:1, KJV)*
I have not come to call the righteous, *but sinners, to repentance. (Luke 5:32, NKJV)*

Please watch this feature about holiness: https://tinyurl.com/5x3whvax

THE SPIRITUAL RACE
RUN FOR YOUR LIFE

Know ye not that they which run in a race run all, but one receiveth the prize? So run, that ye may obtain. (1 Corinthians 9:24, KJV)

Be sober, be vigilant; because your adversary the devil walks about like a roaring lion, seeking whom he may devour. (1 Peter 5:8, NKJV)

*R*un for your life because you are in the world of your enemy. The Lord has allowed the roaring lion, Satan, and his hordes of demons to come after you with temptations to test your loyalty to Him. That statement may sound funny or contrary to popular teachings, but I am serious. Nothing happens in this cosmic expanse unless God allows it, and He has a divine purpose for it. I assure you that not everything He permits in your life will cause your eyes to sparkle or your face to flush with smiles; a jovial word may move you, but the truth will set you free. Brace yourself for the race through life and time.

One school of thought may propose that the soul's race

commences at conception; another, at birth; still another, which I subscribe to, at the moment of accountability. I opted to reason this way and for the same basis that would allow a deceased baby back into Heaven, as it had not rejected God. From the moment the first sin is committed, the soul has demonstrated the capacity to choose life, death, Heaven, or Hell. Therefore, our spiritual competition starts when our free-will engine is cranked up for the first time to process a decision. It is no different from the scenario involving Adam and Eve and the call to decision-making that Joshua demanded of the Israelites.

> Now therefore, fear the LORD, serve Him in sincerity and in truth, and put away the gods which your fathers served on the other side of the River and in Egypt. Serve the LORD! And if it seems evil to you to serve the LORD, **choose for yourselves this day whom you will serve**, whether the gods which your fathers served that were on the other side of the River, or the gods of the Amorites, in whose land you dwell. But as for me and my house, we will serve the LORD. (Joshua 24:14-15, NKJV)

A starting block is a solid piece of rigid material for bracing the feet of a runner at the start of a race

At this point, you may begin to reason about your current state, reflecting on your age and standing with God. Then, you may question when to secure your feet in the starting blocks. I believe God places the soul's feet in the blocks and then fires the starting pistol, a blank handgun that is fired to start track-and-field races. Therefore, today, you are already running, but the pertinent question is, "to where?" There is a narrow road and a broad one. Evidence of your opportunity or assistance to get on or maintain running on the right track is this book in your hand. The narrow road leads heavenward, while the broad, multi-track highway leads to damnation. The dimensions of the broad roadway reveal high capacity requirements, which is similar in concept to the planning performed by transportation engineers throughout the world.

Everyone has a unique, narrow road designed by God that leads to Heaven's gate. Every mile is paved with a type of asphalt called obedience. Despite life's challenges, God wants us to remain on the ordained track because the end will come. Apostle Paul wrote about the race in Hebrews 12:1–2. Matthew 10:37 and Luke 8:14 tell of the type of sacrifice one would have to endure to run the race entirely and successfully. No one can run your race, so run.

> *Therefore we also, since we are surrounded by so great a cloud of witnesses, let us lay aside every weight, and the sin which so easily ensnares us, and let us run with endurance the race that is set before us, looking unto Jesus, the author and finisher of our faith, who for the joy that was set before Him endured the cross, despising the shame, and has sat down at the right hand of the throne of God. (Hebrews 12:1-2, NKJV)*

> *He that loveth father or mother more than me is not worthy of me: and he that loveth son or daughter more than me is not worthy of me. (Matthew 10:37, KJV)*

> *And that which fell among thorns are they, which, when they have heard, go forth, and are choked with cares and riches and pleasures of this life, and bring no fruit to perfection.* (Luke 8:14, KJV)

> *I have fought a good fight, I have finished my course, I have kept the faith.* (2 Timothy 4:7, KJV)

THE JOURNEY'S PRAYER
PURSUING A CONSECRATED HEART

PRAY WITHOUT CEASING

Blessed are the pure in heart, For they shall see God. (Matthew 5:8, NKJV)

Dear Lord,

You said that only the pure in (of) heart would see you and make it back to Heaven.
Therefore, O Lord, please create in me a clean, compassionate heart.
Give me a heart that does not lean on its own understanding but one that trusts in Your Word and promises.
Teach my heart to rely on you, to rest in faith.
Give me a heart that is willing to do your will, to be obedient.
Remove pride and any bitterness from my heart, and replace it with humility, patience, and love.
Reveal all hidden sins, and help me toward forgiveness, correction, and repentance.
Lord, I know you hate sin, but you still love the sinner.

Grant my heart the willingness to pray without ceasing.
Bless my heart to love what you love and hate what you hate.
Bless my heart to be disciplined and consistent in holiness.
Bless my heart to be positive and thankful, and bless my heart to love you and others in Jesus' name, I pray.

Thank you Father.
Amen.

STEP 1 - FORGIVE
AND YOU WILL BE FORGIVEN

WEEK #1

> And be kind to one another, tenderhearted, **forgiving one another, even as God in Christ forgave you.** (Ephesians 4:32, NKJV)

For if you forgive men their trespasses, your heavenly Father will also forgive you. But if you do not forgive men their trespasses, neither will your Father forgive your trespasses. (Matthew 6:14-15 NKJV)

Imagine yourself resting on a bench in a crowded mall, perhaps taking the strain off since you recently had foot surgery. From the stampede of bustling shoppers, a strapping young man loses focus and stumbles when he is right next to you. For a fleeting moment, his entire weight lands on your still-healing foot. You feel a surge of throbbing pain, but he does not even acknowledge you. Now you aren't just in pain; you're also filled with disgust. Unkind and disrespectful behavior makes you angry. Even a muttered apology, however halfhearted, would have lessened your physical and emotional pain, but he didn't bother with that social nicety. You are left with this bitter option: you can forgive him or withhold forgiveness.

Now shift perspective. We are the oblivious mall walkers who lose focus, day after day. We stumble and fall and land on the nail-pierced foot of our Savior, over and over again. And God wants us to tell Him that we're sorry, to acknowledge our misstep.

Forgiveness frequently occurs in both human and divine interactions. Often, its function is to restore the bridge of communication between us and others when sin has blocked and distorted the interpersonal messages we send, which are transmitted in various ways, including verbal, body language, and actions. That bridge doesn't rebuild itself, and the divisive issues can't be ignored. Only the tool of forgiveness can bring about a resolution.

> *And be ye kind one to another, tenderhearted, forgiving one another, even as God for Christ's sake hath forgiven you. (Ephesians 4:32, KJV)*

> *And whenever you stand praying, if you have anything against anyone, forgive him, that your Father in Heaven may also forgive you your trespasses. (Mark 11:25, NKJV)*

SEEK IMMEDIATE FORGIVENESS

In my experience, asking Jesus for forgiveness compels the trespasser to immediately conduct a self-assessment and evaluate the relationship with Jesus just in time to keep it from being strained or broken. Such a quick response also develops reverential fear and results in conscientiousness that prevents recurrences. Who would want to go to God with the same issue every day? Without responsive accountability, the wrong is brushed aside in hopes that it would dissolve into oblivion, but that is an unrealistic expectation.

If you need to forgive anyone, do it now to avoid further division; don't wait till tomorrow. You may forget, but God does not.

> *And if a kingdom be divided against itself, that kingdom cannot stand. And if a house be divided against itself, that house cannot stand. And if Satan rise up against himself, and be divided, he cannot stand, but hath an end. (Mark 3:24-26, KJV)*

Forgiveness helps maintain a structure as a complete whole, even as there is one body, one Spirit, and one life. An unforgiving soul either fails to understand or willfully ignores that it is not an autonomous being that can forfeit forgiving others. It does not own itself nor exist in a vacuum.

> **There is one body, and one Spirit**, *even as ye are called in one hope of your calling; One Lord, one faith, one baptism, One God and Father of all, who is above all, and through all, and in you all. (Ephesians 4:4-6, KJV)*

Without forgiveness, the body of Christ would begin to

disintegrate as the corrosion of disunity and pride eats away at it. Pardoning someone overcomes the human imperfections that would otherwise separate the members and disqualify them from entering the gates of Heaven. Indeed, tolerance, mercy, and social etiquette are foundational for ensuring unity in the body of Christ.

Members of the body of Christ on Earth are an extension of the one in Heaven. Any member who chooses to remain isolated due to unwillingness to forgive has separated itself from its celestial home until reconciliation is attained. This is an unnecessary, crushing weight that will surely sink that soul to the bottom of the eternal abyss if death finds it in an unrepentant state.

If you were lugging a heavyweight, ready to faint under the sweltering midday sun, and someone offered assistance at the critical moment, wouldn't you accept it with delight? Consider another analogy: if you were at the zoo and accidentally fell into the lions' area, how would you feel if someone fearlessly jumped in and carried you to safety? Jesus did much more than shouldering a burden or effecting a rescue. He died for us. Refusing to forgive someone that He died to redeem makes a mockery of His sacrifice. As a result, He is angrily displeased until arrogance is replaced with humility. Strive to maintain an agreeable attitude, recognizing that we are all in Him, although we serve different roles.

> *God judgeth the righteous, and* **God is angry with the wicked [the disobedient] every day.** *(Psalms 7:11, KJV)*

> *[However]* **The Lord is merciful and gracious, slow to anger, and plenteous in mercy.** *He will not always chide: neither will he keep his anger for ever.* **He hath not dealt with us after our sins;** *nor*

rewarded us according to our iniquities. (Psalms 103:8-10, KJV)

AVOID UNFORGIVENESS'S PENALTY

We must seek to pardon or incur a penalty from harboring resentment against someone because that same frame of mind is what we also hold toward God and Jesus. Why should He allow a hater to enter His home or reenter Heaven? Harboring bitterness against another brother or sister is using divine energy to advance the enemy's kingdom, which translates to high treason against the person of Christ. Seeking forgiveness is an act of humility. It expresses guilt, recognizes accountability, and petitions to restore friendship and right standing with God. This is true wisdom, a praiseworthy action that follows the wise virgins' model.

Until forgiveness is sought, the wrong and its associated penalty are on the offender's account, and vengeance is the Lord's. But once it is sought, God will forgive any sin because of His great love. Don't feel shy or worthless. Your life is more than your thoughts—it's worth His life.

> *For You, Lord, are good, **and ready to forgive**, And abundant in mercy to all those who call upon You. (Psalms 86:5, NKJV)*

> *And **when the Lord saw her, he had compassion on her**, and said unto her, Weep not. (Luke 7:13, KJV)*

> *The LORD is slow to anger, and great in power, and will not at all **acquit the wicked**: the LORD hath his way in the whirlwind and in the storm, and the clouds are the dust of his feet. (Nahum 1:3, KJV)*

> *He will turn again, **He will have compassion upon us**; He will subdue our iniquities; and thou wilt cast all their sins into the depths of the sea. (Micah 7:19, KJV)*

> *To me belongeth vengeance, and recompence; **their foot shall slide in due time**: for the day of their calamity is at hand, and the things that shall come upon them make haste. (Deuteronomy 32:35, KJV)*

> *And **I will execute vengeance [if repentance is not sought] in anger and fury upon the heathen**, such as they have not heard. (Micah 5:15, KJV)*

> *But he, **being full of compassion, forgave their iniquity**, and destroyed them not: yea, many a time turned he his anger away, and did not stir up all his wrath. (Psalms 78:38, KJV)*

VERSES ABOUT FORGIVENESS

1. He hath not dealt with us after our sins; nor rewarded us according to our iniquities. For as the Heaven is high above the Earth, so great is his mercy toward them that fear him. As far as the east is from the west, so far hath he removed our transgressions from us. (Psalms 103:10-12, KJV)
2. Then came Peter to him, and said, Lord, how oft shall my brother sin against me, and I forgive him? till seven times? Jesus saith unto him, I say not unto thee, Until seven times: but, Until seventy times seven. (Matthew 18:21-22, KJV)
3. Put on therefore, as the elect of God, holy and

beloved, bowels of mercies, kindness, humbleness of mind, meekness, long-suffering; Forbearing one another, and forgiving one another, if any man have a quarrel against any: even as Christ forgave you, so also do ye. (Colossians 3:12-13, KJV)

DO THIS TODAY AND MAKE IT A LIFESTYLE

1. Recognize that forgiveness is a prerequisite for Heaven.
2. Deliberately forgive all your offenders. Pray blessings in their lives and ask God to remove hurt and bitterness from the hearts of all parties.
3. Determine and practice love for all, especially for those who have wronged you.

SUMMARY POINTS

1. The need for a tool called "forgiveness" implies the existence of problems that need remediation; these issues can't be ignored, nor can they resolve themselves.
2. Forgiveness is used to maintain a structure as a complete whole because there is one body, one Spirit, and one life.
3. Refusing to forgive is disregarding Christ's sacrificial offer of redemption that He died to give everyone.
4. An unforgiving soul either fails to understand or willfully ignores that it is not an autonomous being; it does not own or exist for itself. We have to answer to God.
5. Forgiveness is foundational for ensuring unity in the body of Christ. It overcomes the human imperfections that would otherwise separate the members and disqualify them from entering the gates of Heaven.
6. Without forgiveness, the body of Christ would begin to disintegrate as the corrosion of disunity and pride eats away at it.
7. Members of the body of Christ on Earth are an extension of the one in Heaven. Any member who chooses to remain isolated due to unwillingness to forgive has separated itself from its celestial home.
8. We must seek to pardon, or we will incur a penalty from harboring resentment against someone because that same frame of mind is what we also hold toward God and Jesus.
9. Harboring bitterness against another brother or sister is using divine energy to advance the enemy's

kingdom, which translates to high treason against the person of Christ.
10. Until forgiveness is sought, the wrong and its penalty are on the offender's account, and vengeance is the Lord's.
11. Asking Jesus for forgiveness compels the trespasser to immediately conduct a self-assessment and evaluate the relationship with Jesus just in time to keep it from being strained or broken. This quick response also develops reverential fear and results in conscientiousness that prevents recurrences.

2

STEP 2 - REPENT AND AVOID RECURRENCES

WEEK #2

> The Lord is not slack concerning His promise, as some count slackness, but is long-suffering toward us, not willing that any should perish but **that all should come to repentance.** (2 Peter 3:9 NKJV)

Likewise, I say to you, there is joy in the presence of the angels of God over one sinner who repents. (Luke 15:10, NKJV)

According to *Lifehopeandtruth.com*, repentance is a change of heart and direction. It involves the determination to stop sinning. It is the realization that overcoming sin is a lifelong effort.

Why does our Redeemer want us to forgive and repent promptly? We are entirely responsible for our good and poor choices. His system of divine justice will reward us for each outcome, whether positive or negative. He desires to give us joy, not wanting us to slip into difficulties and excessive pain owing to an unrepentant soul. He wants us to receive eternal life, not death. We can make the reward ceremony easier, even enjoyable, for Him when we live in repentance.

> *For if you return to the LORD, your brethren and your children will be treated with compassion by those who lead them captive, so that they may come back to this land; for the LORD your God is gracious and merciful, and will not turn His face from you if you return to Him. (2 Chronicles 30:9, NKJV)*

A CEASE AND DESIST ORDER

> *And he [John the Baptist] went into all the region around the Jordan, preaching a baptism of repentance for the remission of sins. (Luke 3:3, NKJV)*

Forgiveness and repentance are hand in glove. Repentance begins the effort of regaining focus and applying commitment. If forgiveness were the body of a contract, then repentance is the signer. It puts the agreement into force. It is the equivalent of a cease and desist letter sent to an individual or business, forcing them to stop an allegedly illegal activity and never restart it. Jesus is the spiritual attorney from the court of Heaven, and he is consistently serving wrongdoers with cease and desist orders on behalf of God. Unfortunately, some stubbornly crumple the letter and toss it into the bin—but judgment looms, and God will deal with those who are disrespectful unless his mercy is accepted through repentance.

> For He saith to Moses, ***I will have mercy on whom I will have mercy***, and I will have compassion on whom I will have compassion. (Romans 9:15, KJV)

> **Blessed be the God and Father of our Lord Jesus Christ, who according to His abundant mercy has begotten us again to a living hope through the resurrection of Jesus Christ from the dead, to an inheritance incorruptible and undefiled** and that does not fade away, reserved in Heaven for you, who are kept by the power of God through faith for salvation ready to be revealed in the last time. (1 Peter 1:3-5, NKJV)

While seeking forgiveness is the initial step to obtaining pardon for a wrong, repentance keeps us from becoming repeat offenders on the narrow path back to Heaven. At death, the soul reveals whether it reflects God or the devil. That is the moment of judgement, determining whether the soul is filled with light or darkness, whether that person had seriously repented and had stopped committing wrongs or not, and whether the soul has any interest in Heaven other than wanting to escape the fiery doom of Hell.

For example, suppose the person had asked for forgiveness a thousand times but still habitually committed the wrong? Perhaps they thought that asking for pardon alone was sufficient without committing to ending the wrong. In that case, death will catch the individual unprepared to meet God. They will be like the five foolish virgins, and Hell will be the reward for a lifetime of sin on Earth.

FROM DARKNESS TO LIGHT

Human beings are beautiful and highly sophisticated because they are created in the image of the only wise, invisible, and eternal God. When a soul decides to follow Christ, it is an amazing transformation, a miraculous conversion from darkness to light. However, if a soul continues to pursue a prodigal lifestyle, it drifts further from repentance and descends into greater depths of reprobation. Day by day, the condition of that life becomes even more appalling in the eyes of angels and God, while demons fatten their faces with grins. That is why a soul must be kept clean using the divine disinfectant named repentance.

Repentance means to feel remorse, express regret, and ultimately change from previous wrong behavior. Repentance cleanses the soul, converting it from darkness to light, pulling it out of Hell and placing it in Heavenly places, setting it back on the narrow path to the Kingdom of God. The cleansing agent is the spilled blood of Christ. Only the potency of the blood of Christ can arrest the deterioration caused by sin.

Habitually indulging in sinful deeds enables demonic control over the soul. During that diabolic reign, the soul is technically in Hell (not seated in heavenly places in Christ Jesus), and remains there until the point of repentance. Sin is when one opens the door of their heart to a tempter, and accepts the invitation. Ordinarily, a person cannot merely block demonic attacks while living in sin because the door is already wide open. Repentance closes it. But dying without seeking pardon will render the soul property of the underworld because sin means darkness, and darkness cannot coexist in Heaven, the home of light.

But God, who is rich in mercy, because of His great love with which He loved us, even when we were dead in

> trespasses, made us alive together with Christ (by grace you have been saved), and raised us up together, and made us sit together in the heavenly places in Christ Jesus. (Ephesians 2:4-6, NKJV)

DELAYING REPENTANCE

Repentance should be timely; one must act *now* because tomorrow is not promised to anyone. I suspect many of the souls now eternally lost to Hell would have changed if they had more time . . . but their time ran out. The time you have is an opportunity.

> *The future is something which everyone reaches at the rate of sixty minutes an hour, whatever he does, whoever he is. – C.S. Lewis*

> *Better three hours too soon than a minute too late. – William Shakespeare.*

> *Lost time is never found again. – Benjamin Franklin.*

> *The key is in not spending time, but in investing it. – Stephen R. Covey.*

> **Boast not thyself of tomorrow;** *for thou knowest not what a day may bring forth. (Proverbs 27:1, KJV)*

> **Take therefore no thought for the morrow,** *for the morrow shall take thought for the things of itself. Sufficient unto the day is the evil thereof. (Matthew 6:34, KJV)*

A WINDOW OF OPPORTUNITY

Time is grace-inspired, the window of opportunity that intentionally ticks away. Aligning with a window of opportunity is crucial and failure to do so can be very costly, as an example from NASA proves:

> *The spacecraft had originally tried to reach the planet in 2010 but was sent off to orbit the sun instead after the death of one of its engines. After that setback, the spacecraft bided its time until another window of opportunity would present itself to make a move. And such a day came, exactly five years later.*
>
> — SPACE.COM

A lifetime is a personal and unique window of opportunity, and time is only available and applicable on Earth. It doesn't exist in Hell, nor does it exist in Heaven. Time is measurable; it does not have the fundamentally godlike attribute that makes it eternal or everlasting. It has limits. Every tick of the clock carries the sinning soul deeper into the abyss or raises the repentant soul to loftier heights.

Seeking forgiveness is verbal and conceptual, but repentance is action-oriented. The soul or person has to live out the heart change before God, angels, other humans, and demons—because they are all watching us. The angels are watching to help and cheer us on, while the demons are surveilling us and strategizing their next assault. Of course, God is observing with a loving heart and planning ways to keep the person from all dangers, spiritual and physical, but we must also pray so we will be able to defeat the attacks. Furthermore, God has to allow scope for free-will to operate.

The challenge is to accept this truth: above all, true repentance, which means stopping the wrong and not restarting it, is an effective commitment to God and one's eternal life. It demonstrates a Heaven-pleasing level of seriousness against sin. Otherwise, any confession, verbal or otherwise, is a mockery, and God will not be mocked. Repent today to escape God's wrath against sin.

> **Be not deceived; God is not mocked: for whatsoever a man soweth, that shall he also reap.** *For he that soweth to his flesh shall of the flesh reap corruption; but he that soweth to the Spirit shall of the Spirit reap life everlasting. And let us not be weary in well doing: for in due season we shall reap, if we faint not. As we have therefore opportunity, let us do good unto all men, especially unto them who are of the household of faith. (Galatians 6:7-10, KJV)*

> **The LORD shall send upon thee cursing, vexation, and rebuke**, *in all that thou settest thine hand unto for to do, until thou be destroyed, and until thou perish quickly; because of the wickedness of thy doings, whereby thou hast forsaken me. (Deuteronomy 28:20, KJV)*

> *Go to now, ye that say, today or tomorrow we will go into such a city, and continue there a year, and buy and sell, and get gain:* **Whereas ye know not what shall be on the morrow.** *For what is your life? It is even a vapor, that appeareth for a little time, and then vanisheth away. For that ye ought to say, If the Lord will, we shall live, and do this, or that. (James 4:13-15, KJV)*

> *Therefore we ought to give the more earnest heed to the things which we have heard, lest at any time we should let them slip. For if the word spoken by angels was stedfast, and every transgression and disobedience received a just recompense of reward; How shall we escape, if we neglect so great salvation; which at the first began to be spoken by the Lord, and was confirmed unto us by them that heard him; God also bearing them witness, both with signs and wonders, and with divers miracles, and gifts of the Holy Ghost, according to his own will? (Hebrews 2:1-4, KJV)*

VERSES ABOUT REPENTANCE

1. The Lord is not slack concerning his promise, as some men count slackness; but is long-suffering to us-ward, not willing that any should perish, but that all should come to repentance. (2 Peter 3:9, KJV)
2. If My people who are called by My name will humble themselves, and pray and seek My face, and turn from their wicked ways [or repent], then I will hear from Heaven, and will forgive their sin and heal their land. (2 Chronicles 7:14, NKJV)
3. Repent therefore and be converted, that your sins may be blotted out, so that times of refreshing may come from the presence of the Lord. (Acts 3:19, NKJV)
4. Then Peter said unto them, Repent, and be baptized every one of you in the name of Jesus Christ for the remission of sins, and ye shall receive the gift of the Holy Ghost. (Acts 2:38, KJV)

DO THIS TODAY AND MAKE IT A LIFESTYLE

1. Consider your deeds and thoughts that are displeasing to God. Tell Him you are sorry for using His life and time in such an inefficient manner and ask Him to strengthen you against recurrences.
2. Perform an online or offline bible search for references to repentance and study them.
3. Realize that it's not enough to say, "I repent." A behavior change must follow those words. Otherwise, the effort is merely lip service.

SUMMARY POINTS

1. Repentance is equivalent to a cease and desist letter sent to an individual or business to stop allegedly illegal activity and not to restart it.
2. Repentance means to feel remorse, express regret, and ultimately change from a previous wrongdoing. Repentance cleanses the soul, converting it from darkness to light.
3. If forgiveness was the body of a contract, then repentance is the signer. It puts the agreement into force.
4. If a soul continues to pursue a prodigal lifestyle, it drifts further from repentance and descends into greater depths of reprobation. Day by day, the condition of that life becomes even more appalling in the eyes of angels and God. The soul must be kept clean using the divine disinfectant of repentance.
5. Habitually indulging in sinful deeds enables demonic control over the soul. During that demonic reign, the soul is technically in Hell, and remains there until the point of repentance.
6. Repentance must be timely; one must act upon it now because tomorrow is not promised to anyone.
7. Seeking forgiveness is verbal and conceptual, but repentance is action-oriented. The soul or person has to live out the heart change before God, angels, other humans, and demons—because they are all watching us.
8. True repentance, which means stopping the wrong and not restarting it, is a practical commitment to God and one's eternal life. It demonstrates a Heaven-

pleasing level of seriousness against sin or wanting to reenter Heaven.

3

STEP 3 - PRAY AND FAST AND LET GOD'S WILL BE DONE

WEEK #3

> **Call to Me, and I will answer you,** and show you great and mighty things, which you do not know. (Jeremiah 33:3, NKJV)

***Pray without ceasing**, in everything give thanks; for this is the will of God in Christ Jesus for you. (1 Thessalonians 5:17-18, NKJV)*

When I, an imperfect creature, don't pray, I become sloppy and begin to slide, accelerated in my disgrace by the same thoughts and desires from which God, through Jesus, has rescued me. Through the years, I have realized that aspirations, sound reasoning, and admirable intentions are only practice sessions for the marathon through life and time to Heaven. However, completing this long-distance task demands practical discipline and consistent dedication; only this will amount to the resistance necessary to counter the allure of surrendering to procrastination and complacency.

> *And because lawlessness will abound, the love of many will grow cold. But he who endures to the end shall be saved. (Matthew 24:12-13, NKJV)*

Imperfection is the sobering truth that we need help and are not self-sustaining. We sin every day, in thoughts, deeds, or both. Therefore, asking for forgiveness and setting one's heart to seek repentance is a commendable and required effort. Since "once saved always saved" is a fairy tale, we must pursue forgiveness and repentance to address each wrong. By singling out and identifying each trespass and handling it individually with prayer, we can monitor against relapses. Prayer is how we call out for assistance to remain spiritually healthy as we work on our qualification for Heaven. We use free will to decide whether to pray or not, so choose like a wise virgin. Pray according to God's will; otherwise, you may get what you ask for even though it is not His will, and that could be disastrous.

EFFICIENT USE OF FREE WILL

> **Watch ye and pray, lest ye enter into temptation.**
> *The spirit truly is ready, but the flesh is weak.*
> *(Mark 14:38, KJV)*

> *And when he was at the place, he said unto them,* **Pray that ye enter not into temptation.** *(Luke 22:40, KJV)*

STEP 3 - PRAY AND FAST | 175

Free will creates a blockade that prevents God from intervening in our lives without an invitation, and that express invitation is issued through prayer. Free will is like a privacy blind, and God respects that right to seclusion, but it only lasts for a lifetime. Let's use it productively because the Lord loves a profit; He does not want to lose anyone. When we forgive others, turn from sin, and pray, that's profitable to God and us and results in a loss for the enemy.

> And **cast ye the unprofitable servant into outer darkness;** there shall be weeping and gnashing of teeth. (Matthew 25:30, KJV)
>
> Thus says the Lord, your Redeemer, The Holy One of Israel: **I am the Lord your God, Who teaches you to profit**, Who leads you by the way you should go. (Isaiah 48:17, NKJV)

Prayer is the humble application of free will to form a tactical relationship with Heaven against oppressive influences from the underworld. It is a divine strategy to promote a healthy soul and body and builds a spiritual community. God is delighted when a person prays deliberately and consistently, pleading for divine mercy, guidance, protection, and strength to fight the good fight.

> **Fight the good fight of faith, lay hold on eternal life,** whereunto thou art also called, and hast professed a good profession before many witnesses. (1 Timothy 6:12, KJV)

If we don't pray but still expect God to answer our hearts' unspoken yearnings, any expectation for a favorable result is unrealistic for two reasons. Firstly, we would be anticipating that He would override our free will. God cannot change. He also told us to "Ask, and it will be given . . ." Secondly, He would take care of all unspoken requests universally and act similarly every time to be reasonable to all. The sheer scope of that level of involvement would nullify the purpose of giving us the power to choose. Indeed, under those circumstances, a person would not be allowed to decide for or against God. There would be no need for the person to be on Earth in the first place or for Jesus to die on a cross. Finally, prayer influences the outcome of many events, and that is why we should pray without ceasing.

> ***Pray without ceasing.*** *(1 Thessalonians 5:17, KJV)*

> *And **He spake a parable unto them to this end, that men ought always to pray, and not to faint**; Saying, There was in a city a judge, which feared not God, neither regarded man: And there was a widow in that city; and she came unto him, saying, Avenge me of mine adversary. And he would not for a while: but afterward he said within himself, Though I fear not God, nor regard man; Yet because this widow troubleth me, I will avenge her, lest by her continual coming she weary me. And the Lord said, Hear what the unjust judge saith. And shall not God avenge his own elect, which cry day and night unto him, though he bear long with them? I tell you that he will avenge them speedily. Nevertheless when the Son of man cometh, shall he find faith on the Earth? (Luke 18:1-8, KJV)*

Without free will, there would be no need to pray because God would have complete access and control over each soul's behaviors. If He assumed full leadership of all of His images, then there would be no need for His death, the world would be different from what it is today, and you and I wouldn't be connecting through this guide. Although God is all-powerful and omnipresent, He has allowed humans to choose to join Him in Heaven or reject Him. Because we wrestle against invisible, demonic influencers, the stakes are high, and we need constant assistance. A constant need for assistance means a continual need for prayer.

THE POWER OF WORDS

Words are living agents that produce a cause-and-effect outcome with each utterance, irrespective of motive. For instance, saying "I cannot do anything correctly" might be overly modest, but the declaration can be destructive in the spiritual sphere, where the soul resides and operates. A more pointed example is in Luke 23:3: "And Pilate asked him, saying, Art thou the King of the Jews? And he answered him and said, Thou sayest it." The keywords are "Thou sayest it." Although Pilate asked a question, but Jesus responded as if it was a confession; whether the words were structured as an inquiry or an outright statement, the impact was the same because words are living agents that promote life or death.

> *Wherefore, my beloved brethren, let every man be swift to hear, slow to speak, slow to wrath. (James 1:19, KJV)*

In 1 Thessalonians, we are commanded to pray without ceasing, so neglecting to pray is an act of disobedience. Petitioning is the word-based protocol to request divine help. Praying to God demonstrates respect for Him, for His existence and power. Prayer is more than just saying a bunch of words because words have spiritual power for good or evil. God used words to create everything. Moreover, He is the Word.

And the Word became flesh and dwelt among us, and we beheld His glory, the glory as of the only begotten of the Father, full of grace and truth. (John 1:14, NKJV)

We are supported or destroyed by words. For example, on Judgment Day, people will hear these words:

*His lord said unto him, **well done, thou good and faithful servant:** thou hast been faithful over a few things, I will make thee ruler over many things: **enter thou into the joy of thy lord**. (Matthew 25:21, KJV)*

OR

*And then will I profess unto them, **I never knew you: depart from me**, ye that work iniquity. (Matthew 7:23, KJV)*

Words are a powerful spiritual tool for constructing or deconstructing someone, starting with the soul. Spiritual damages or repairs might not be visible in the physical realm, in the body, but they are still present in the soul. The Bible gives us many warnings about the use of words:

***Let no corrupt communication proceed out of your mouth**, but that which is good to the use of edifying, that it may minister grace unto the hearers. (Ephesians 4:29, KJV)*

***Death and life are in the power of the tongue:** and they that love it shall eat the fruit thereof. (Proverbs 18:21, KJV)*

Be careful for nothing, but in every thing by prayer

> ***and supplication*** *with thanksgiving let your requests be made known unto God. (Philippians 4:6, KJV)*

> *And he spake a parable unto them to this end, that **men [everyone] ought always to pray**, and not to faint. (Luke 18:1, KJV)*

We support and promote life when the words we speak are consistent with biblical precepts. For instance, if we say "I can do all things through Christ who strengthens me" instead of "I will never accomplish this mission," we soothe the anxieties of our hearts and endorse life, not death. Indeed, Jesus wants us to illustrate our agreement with Him as we pray, by speaking or confessing as He does.

PRAYING THROUGH THE BIBLE

An effective approach to improving our habit of prayer is to be diligent in reading the Bible. When we have a greater understanding of the Holy Writ, our expectations and prayers will align with divine expectations and the will of God. On the other hand, God may grant a petitioner's wish, but the results may not align with His will, which can prove disastrous.

Still, even if we have little knowledge of the Bible, God wants us to come to Him boldly. We can stand unashamed before Him, use plain language to communicate our thoughts and wishes, acknowledge our sins, seek forgiveness, and intentionally abstain from anything that challenges His holiness. By following these guidelines, we will fashion useful prayers, experience spiritual growth, and, most of all, please Him.

WHY WE SHOULD PRAY

> *Truly, truly, I say to you, whoever believes in me will also do the works that I do; and greater works than these will he do, because I am going to the Father.* ***Whatever you ask in my name, this I will do, that the Father may be glorified in the Son. If you ask me anything in my name, I will do it.*** *(John 14:12-14, ESV)*
>
> *And He told them a parable to the effect that they ought always to* ***pray and not lose heart.*** *(Luke 18:1, ESV)*

Why should we pray? We have spiritual enemies that are invisible to our natural eyes. They are very cunning and utterly Hell-bent on destroying us. They are zealous in instigating us to do anything that would provoke God to anger. Their mission is to prevent souls from getting back to Heaven, and they are very skilled in their pursuit. The Bible describes these enemies as "rulers of the darkness" and as a "roaring lion."

> *For we wrestle not against flesh and blood, but against principalities, against powers, against the rulers of the darkness of this world, against spiritual wickedness in high places. (Ephesians 6:12, KJV)*
>
> *Be sober, be vigilant; because your* ***adversary the devil****, as a roaring lion, walketh about, seeking whom he may devour. (1 Peter 5:8, KJV)*

Because God cannot change, we must, or we will never

measure up to His standard. That requires sacrificial effort, so we need to pray for strength and focus. When we pray, we practice discipline against demonic spirits of complacency and compromise. They're not merely emotional or psychological misfits; they are high-order dark forces eternally bent on picking souls off the narrow path re-routing them to eternal doom.

At this point, I would like to share a personal story about the danger of compromising. Compromise is more than a disruption of social or relationship-based integrity or a question about morality; it trivializes and ignores things of spiritual significance. I urge you to pray against the lure of compromise and complacency.

My lesson began the evening of the day I had devoted to fasting. The Holy Spirit, who speaks to us in unspoken but certain ways, nudged me to continue the fast by skipping the eagerly anticipated evening meal, but hunger can speak in a very commanding voice. Instead of obeying, I yielded to the voice of hunger, continued to fix myself a sandwich, and proceeded to eat it. Truthfully, I had doubts about my decision. God's expectation was made abundantly clear when I received an unexpected text message from my prophetic friend. He wrote: "No compromise. Compromise equals demise." That was the second time in about two weeks I had gotten such a warning.

As I pondered this message, I decided to check a dictionary and thesaurus. To my dismay, the first two synonyms I saw for compromise were "negotiate" and "bargain." Right away, I knew that I was guilty of disobedience. You see, it had been a good day, a day I had done something for the Lord, so I reckoned that despite the prompting of the Spirit, I was justified to have the meal because of what I had already done for Him. I was attempting to compromise with the Creator of Heaven and Earth, to bargain with Him. I did not commit the sin doggedly, but the act was still sinful anyway, and God does not tolerate any degree of disobedience.

The lesson here is that we must be fully aware that God does not invite humankind into His decision-making. When He issues a command, we are to obey without questioning. After all, how can imperfect beings question Perfection?

If we don't listen to the Holy Spirit by responding with obedience, Acts 7:51 may become the verdict against us. This verse describes the Israelites' stubbornness after God has mercifully delivered them from 400 years of captivity.

> *Ye stiff-necked and uncircumcised in heart and ears,*
> *ye do always resist the Holy Ghost, as your fathers*
> *did, so do ye. (Acts 7:51, KJV)*

The demonic influences behind complacency and compromise work as a team, and they will tempt and destroy the soul if their stealthy maneuvers are not readily spotted and managed. Complacency is the stage builder: it places the potential victim onto the podium of smugness, self-righteousness, and gratification.

Next, the spirit of compromise or trade-off arrives on the platform. The vulnerable soul is now seated with confidence and presented with appealing, reasonable, and even justifiable options. Nonetheless, the bargain-making spirits' proposal is the opposite of what is pleasing to God. It becomes a god and receives the glory and worship owed to the true God. That idolatry could lead a soul to Hell if forgiveness and repentance are not sought. Therefore, we pray against the spirit or influence of idolatry.

> *But the fearful, and unbelieving, and the abominable,*
> *and murderers, and whoremongers, and sorcerers,*
> *and **idolaters**, and all liars, shall have their part in*

> the lake which burneth with fire and brimstone, which is the second death. (Revelation 21:8, KJV)

> I will remove your carved images and sacred pillars from you so that you will no longer worship the work of your hands. (Micah 5:13, CSB)

A MAINTENANCE STRATEGY

> And he said to them, which of you who has a friend will go to him at midnight and say to him, 'Friend, lend me three loaves, for a friend of mine has arrived on a journey, and I have nothing to set before him'; and he will answer from within, 'Do not bother me; the door is now shut, and my children are with me in bed. I cannot get up and give you anything'? I tell you, though he will not get up and give him anything because he is his friend, yet because of his impudence he will rise and give him whatever he needs. And **I tell you, ask, and it will be given to you; seek, and you will find; knock, and it will be opened to you. For everyone who asks receives, and the one who seeks finds, and to the one who knocks it will be opened.** What father among you, if his son asks for a fish, will instead of a fish give him a serpent; or if he asks for an egg, will give him a scorpion? I (Luke 11:5-12, ESV)

> **Note:** We know that God does not listen to sinners [He first wants us to turn to doing right, but we can call upon Him to save us], but if anyone is a worshiper of God and does his will, God listens to him. (John 9:31, ESV)

> *If my people who are called by my name **humble themselves, and pray and seek my face and turn from their wicked ways**, then I will hear from heaven and will forgive their sin and heal their land.* (2 Chronicles 7:14, ESV)

> ***The eyes of the Lord are on the righteous and His ears are open to their request.*** *But the face of the Lord is against those who do what is evil.* (1 Peter 3:12, HCSB)

> *And **let us not grow weary of doing good, for in due season we will reap, if we do not give up.*** (Galatians 6:9, ESV)

The act of prayer demonstrates an understanding that the soul needs support or maintenance from its Creator. Failing to pray is like buying a new car and driving it without ever taking it for a tune-up or an oil change.

We also pray because sin is crushing, not only in Hell but also on the Earth. We don't immediately feel its full impact or weight because of grace. Grace is a divine moment in time that restrains sin's weightiness and grants the souls an opportunity to reconcile to God. Grace alone allows us to pray for forgiveness and live a repentant life. Otherwise, the full weight of accumulated sin is waiting to saddle the soul for eternity in Hell.

Meanwhile, demons constantly try to burst through the spiritual veil that keeps them at bay. Their attacks could cause both spiritual and physical harm. Demons might even enter an animal or person to assault us. We rarely know about those plans because we are not part of that decision process, but that is why the Bible encourages us to pray nonstop for God's protection.

We pray not only against external attacks and temptations,

but also for the strength to endure divine testing and the wisdom to understand our hearts' inclinations.

> **The heart is deceitful above all things,** *and desperately wicked: who can know it? (Jeremiah 17:9, KJV)*

> *But God hath revealed them unto us by his Spirit, for the Spirit searcheth all things, yea, the deep things of God.* **For what man knoweth the things of a man, save the spirit of man which is in him?** *even so the things of God knoweth no man, but the Spirit of God. (1 Corinthians 2:10-11, KJV)*

> **Create in me a clean heart,** *O God; and renew a right spirit within me. Cast me not away from thy presence; and take not thy holy spirit from me. (Psalms 51:10-11, KJV)*

Our knowledge is minimal. Compared to the boundless insight of those not restricted by the flesh, such as the devil and the other fallen angels, we have minds like children.

Although we have an unbounded capacity for knowledge in the soul, living on Earth, in the flesh, places us into a relatively limited state even though our adversary has full supernatural capabilities. Once we accept this great, sobering truth, we begin to understand our dependence on God and his angels. Each soul is responsible for praying every day—every morning, noon, and night—each week, month, and year.

On the other hand, neglecting to pray is the equivalent of someone blocking a father from seeing his child, even though he has full custody. That equivalent spiritual violation is painful to God, and He will take revenge if the offender does not pursue forgiveness and repentance to repair any breach.

We are His children, and He is a Good Parent. He is the perfect Father, so He will surely assist His children when they seek Him in prayer. Still, I must offer a word of caution. God is perfect in love, and as such, it is intolerable to Him when we try to exploit His compassion with the ill-advised perception that He must answer any prayer we hurl heavenward. We must respect the fact that God has feelings, too. In other words, the most effective prayers are from righteous people, those who have surrendered their lives to Christ to manage it safely back to Heaven.

> *Confess your trespasses to one another, and pray for one another, that you may be healed.* ***The effective, fervent prayer of a righteous man avails much.***
> *(James 5:16, NKJV)*

The effectiveness of prayer depends on the cleanliness or readiness of the petitioner's soul to receive the answer. For example, a person still living in sin is like an old wineskin, incapable of storing new wine without leaking or breaking. The old wineskin example is also a point about the mercy and love of God for everyone. It is not that He does not want to help the unrepentant person or soul; it is just that the person is not ready nor can receive some divine gifts. Moreover, the Bible likens the mismatch or unpreparedness to casting pearls before swine.

> *No man putteth a piece of new cloth unto an old garment, for that which is put in to fill it up taketh from the garment, and the rent is made worse.* ***Neither do men put new wine into old bottles, else the bottles break, and the wine runneth out, and the bottles perish***, *but they put new wine into*

new bottles, and both are preserved. (Matthew 9:16-17, KJV)

Give not that which is holy unto the dogs, neither cast ye your pearls before swine, *lest they trample them under their feet, and turn again and rend you. (Matthew 7:6, KJV)*

DETERMINATION IS REQUIRED

*And shall God not avenge His own elect **who cry out day and night** [in persistence] to Him, though He bears long with them? (Luke 18:7, NKJV)*

*If any of you lacks wisdom [or anything], let him ask God, who gives generously to all without reproach, and it will be given him. But **let him ask in faith, with no doubting, for the one who doubts is like a wave of the sea that is driven and tossed by the wind. For that person must not suppose that he will receive anything from the Lord;** he is a double-minded man, unstable in all his ways. (James 1:5-8, ESV)*

It takes discipline to be consistently prayerful. Online research shows that more than 85% of workers hate their jobs. Many undergo various types of abuse and endure different types of discomfort in the workplace. Yet, they dutifully bear up under duress each day to earn what is needed to feed themselves.

In contrast to the physical work-life, souls will exist forever (in Heaven or Hell), yet most people do little spiritual upkeep.

Seeking forgiveness, living a repentant life, and praying are the means to keep the soul alive; without these, the soul would die of spiritual malnutrition. The sad part is that many don't see the internal devastation until it is too late, and their souls are doomed for eternity. That is why we must live by faith today, to understand and trust that God is working out everything for our good. Still, we must work with Him as well. Continue to pray.

> And **we know that all things work together for good to them that love God**, to them who are the called according to his purpose. (Romans 8:28, KJV)

The promise of Romans 8:28 is not directed to everyone. It is only promised to those who love the Lord. Yes, many will raise hands confidently, proclaiming their love for Jesus, but what does it mean to love the Lord? Obedience is the only verifiable expression of love for Christ. Anything else is lip service or hypocrisy.

> *This people draweth nigh unto me with their mouth, and honoreth me with their lips; **but their heart is far from me**. (Matthew 15:8, KJV)*

> *He who has My commandments and keeps them, it is he who loves Me. And he who loves Me will be loved by My Father, and I will love him and manifest Myself to him. (John 14:21, NKJV)*

> *If you love Me, keep My commandments. (John 14:15, NKJV)*

We pray against temptations because they are prompts from the underworld to destroy our souls. Temptation is not merely an enticement; it is a deliberate deathtrap. It incentivizes or encourages the soul to do something sinful or immoral. However, we pray for strength to endure times of testing. Compare to a temptation, a trial or test has a nurturing and redemptive quality because it is meant to determine a person's proficiency or deficiency. Improvement is the objective. God constructs a test to help us recognize our weaknesses. Once we realize and accept our mortal shortfalls, He expects us to turn and continue in prayer for the sustenance and power we need to bridge the spiritual divide that is separating us from His will. Remember, God tests, but devils tempt.

> *Watch and pray,* ***that ye enter not into temptation:*** *the spirit indeed is willing, but the flesh is weak.* (Matthew 26:41, KJV)

> ***Let no one say when he is tempted, "I am tempted by God";*** *for God cannot be tempted by evil, nor does He Himself tempt anyone.* (James 1:13, NKJV)

AN EFFECTIVE PRAYER METHOD

Perhaps you are new to praying and need to know what to pray about. I believe it might be best for you to start by praying for wisdom and strength to overcome the temptations that caused Eve and Adam to fall. First, tell God that you are sorry for all your sins and ask for forgiveness. Next, pray against the lust of the flesh, the lust of the eyes, and the pride of life, accordingly. Make a list of what you remember and ask for pardon as you move through the list. See the section, "7 Prayers for the Journey."

> *Love not the world, neither the things that are in the world. If any man love the world, the love of the Father is not in him.* ***For all that is in the world,***

> *the lust of the flesh, and the lust of the eyes, and the pride of life, is not of the Father, but is of the world. And the world passeth away, and the lust thereof: but he that doeth the will of God abideth forever.* (1 John 2:15-17, KJV)

> *Whereby are given unto us exceeding great and precious promises, that by these ye might be partakers of the divine nature, having* **escaped the corruption that is in the world through lust.** *(2 Peter 1:4, KJV)*

Any prayer expression that seeks reconciliation with our Heavenly Father is a tremendous blessing because you are talking to the King of kings and the only Redeemer or Rescuer of our souls. But the model prayer is perhaps the best of all because the person Who answers it is the one who taught it to us.

> *Our Father which art in Heaven, Hallowed be thy name. Thy kingdom come. Thy will be done in Earth, as it is in Heaven. Give us this day our daily bread. And forgive us our debts, as we forgive our debtors. And lead us not into temptation, but deliver us from evil: For thine is the kingdom, and the power, and the glory, forever. Amen.* (Matthew 6:9-13, KJV)

FASTING

> *Then I proclaimed a fast there at the river of Ahava, that we might humble ourselves before our God, to*

> *seek from Him the right way for us and our little ones and all our possessions. (Ezra 8:21, NKJV)*

One way of drawing closer to the Lord is to conduct a **consecration**. I call it a "consecration fast," although abstinence from food is not the challenge in this example. Instead, the call to action is a week-long commitment to spending at least one hour a day in prayer and Bible reading. After you have met that successfully for at least seven days, the consecration fast continues to challenge you to repeat that level of commitment every week. This practice, or something similar, is expected for the followers of Christ to maintain spiritual health.

If praying is like a mini sacrifice to God because it requires time and discipline, fasting is the major one. Overcoming the agitating pulsations of hunger is one aspect of the challenge; wrestling with what seems to be an onslaught of demonic opposition is the other. Restraining a sustained and compelling desire to satisfy hunger requires self-control and a mission-oriented mindset. But fasting can be rewarding, producing results that significantly dwarf those realized by prayer alone.

> *And wherever it seizes him, it throws him down; he foams at the mouth, gnashes his teeth, and becomes rigid. **So I spoke to Your disciples, that they should cast it out, but they could not.** (Mark 9:18, NKJV)*

> *So He said to them, **This kind can come out by nothing but prayer and fasting.** (Mark 9:29, NKJV)*

Another example of fasting's efficacy is Daniel's three-week fast. The following verses provide an account of the need to offer our bodies as living sacrifices on the altar of fasting because our enemies are unimaginably persistent in attending to our destruction. Can you imagine that although Daniel received his answer on day one, he had to struggle for twenty-one days until Archangel Michael's intervention warded off the diabolic hindrances?

> *I beseech you therefore, brethren, by the mercies of God,* ***that ye present your bodies a living sacrifice, holy, acceptable unto God, which is your reasonable service.*** *And be not conformed to this world: but be ye transformed by the renewing of your mind, that ye may prove what is that good, and acceptable, and perfect, will of God. (Romans 12:1-2, KJV)*

> *In those days I, Daniel, was mourning three full weeks. I ate no pleasant food, no meat or wine came into my mouth, nor did I anoint myself at all, till three whole weeks were fulfilled. (Daniel 10:2-3, NKJV)*

> *Then he said to me,* ***do not fear, Daniel, for from the first day that you set your heart to understand, and to humble yourself before your God, your words were heard****; and I have come because of your words.* ***But the prince of the kingdom of Persia withstood me twenty-one days;*** *and behold, Michael, one of the chief princes, came to help me, for I had been left alone there with the kings of Persia. (Daniel 10:12-13, NKJV)*

BENEFITS OF FASTING

Fasting is an opportunity to demote self appropriately, reduce pride, reduce the darkness in our hearts with the light of God's presence, and demonstrate a willingness to obtain heavenly virtues. Just as Jesus made Himself the perfect sacrifice by offering up His sinless life on the cross, we present our bodies to Him as a living sacrifice by denying ourselves the pleasure and joy of eating.

Fasting is primarily effective from a soul bent on holiness, one that is willing to shift from darkness to light through the spiritual progress known as repentance. The fervent prayer of a righteous man avails much, and the fasting of holy people is profitable. Therefore, when you are ready to commit to uprightness, ask for forgiveness, then begin your fast.

Fasting may even cause your body to lose some weight, although that should not motivate you to undertake this discipline. But even more rewarding is that your soul sheds weight as well. Unpardoned sins, which are dark like spiritual grime, weigh heavily on the soul. Fasting and praying for a higher level of sanctity, especially when directed by God, will invite the Holy Spirit in and provide the opportunity for Him to clean the soul and flush out the darkness. Under such circumstances, the Spirit's workings may result in supernatural experiences such as visions and healing. Demons may even be cast out!

> *But this kind of demon won't leave unless you have prayed and gone without food. (Matthew 17:21, TLB)*

Fasting draws someone into a unique, intimate relationship with Christ. Still, the challenge is, one must be prepared to deny oneself from the most common pleasure on the Earth. Typically, abstaining from food is an exercise in subjecting the body to suffer, to burn the fuel of self-denial while enhancing the attitude of worship. This is similar to how a fire reduces the wick and wax to light a room or how a smelting furnace's intense heat separates pure gold from the dross. In other words, we draw closer to God when our pride-prone selves are reduced by fasting.

There is a special consideration that all those who fast should keep in mind. Fasting is a type of worship, not leeway to unthinkingly request favors from God. He is not a slot machine. Reverence and willingness to submit to his will must supersede all expectations. Therefore, a misguided perception that fasting for 40 days, for example, would be more productive or pleasing to God than, say, five days is prideful, and pride is the foul-smelling odor of a soul that would cause God to resist it.

On our own, we fallen beings cannot muster any effort worthy of Heaven's attention. But humility and submission to the magnificence of Christ are the pathways to a profitable, Heaven-approved fast. At times, God will nudge us to enter spiritual combat at a higher level, bolstered by the privilege of fasting.

In my experience, a God-initiated fast is usually more challenging and raises a more profound sense of sacrifice than when the decision to fast is entirely mine. Perhaps the reason for the increased challenge is that the undertaking is now not only about the fast; it is also about the compounded weight of obedience. In other words, fasting seems harder for me when God is leading. Perhaps it is my fallen Adamic nature opting for autonomy.

All in all, fasting is good for spiritual growth, self-control, and physical health, but one must always fast with a respectful attitude and expectation. For instance, don't fast with the impolite and dogged mindset that "I have completed my portion, and Jesus should do His part now." Let patience guide your interactions with Him. Humbly surrender to His will. God is sovereign, so a puny human cannot compel Him to do anything. He owes us nothing, but everything He does for us is done out of love.

> *Is this not the fast that I have chosen: To loose the bonds of wickedness, To undo the heavy burdens, To let the oppressed go free, And that you break every yoke? Is it not to share your bread with the hungry, And that you bring to your house the poor who are cast out; When you see the naked, that you cover him, And not hide yourself from your own flesh?* (Isaiah 58:6-7, NKJV)

VERSES ABOUT PRAYING AND FASTING

1. Pray without ceasing. In every thing give thanks: for this is the will of God in Christ Jesus concerning you. (1 Thessalonians 5:17-18, KJV)
2. In this manner, therefore, pray: Our Father in Heaven, Hallowed be Your name. Your kingdom come. Your will be done On Earth as it is in Heaven. Give us this day our daily bread. And forgive us our debts, As we forgive our debtors. And do not lead us into temptation, But deliver us from the evil one. For Yours is the kingdom and the power and the glory forever. Amen. (Matthew 6:9-13, NKJV)
3. Being forty days tempted of the devil. And in those days he did eat nothing: and when they were ended, he afterward hungered. (Luke 4:2, KJV)
4. And when they had ordained them elders in every church, and had prayed with fasting, they commended them to the Lord, on whom they believed. (Acts 14:23, KJV)

DO THIS TODAY AND MAKE IT A LIFESTYLE

1. Seek earnestly to pray at least twice a day, morning and evening.
2. Make a list of prayer points and try to spend at least 10-20 minutes with your Heavenly Father each time. He likes the company.
3. Determine to dedicate at least one day to fasting per week, perhaps from morning to later afternoon. You may drink water only, abstain from all solid consumption, or use some other combination. Use some or all of the time to meditate, pray, and study the Bible.

SUMMARY POINTS

1. Prayer is how we call out for assistance to remain spiritually healthy, qualified for Heaven.
2. When we forgive others, turn from sin, and pray, that's profitable to God and us and results in a loss for the enemy
3. We are commanded to pray without ceasing, so neglecting to pray is an act of disobedience.
4. Praying for others demonstrates our love for Jesus. Prayer is an engagement with Him. It maintains our friendship with Him and helps preserve the Father-child relationship.
5. Prayer is the humble application of free will to form a tactical relationship with Heaven against oppressive influences from the underworld.
6. If we don't pray but still expect God to answer our hearts' unspoken yearnings, any expectation for a favorable result is unrealistic.
7. Jesus wants us to illustrate our agreement with Him as we pray, by speaking or confessing as He does. An effective approach to improving our habit of prayer is to be diligent in reading the Bible.
8. Though we are encouraged to pray for our desires, we must be wise about our requests. God may grant a petitioner's wish, but the results may not align with His will, so we need to pray that we will know His will.
9. We have spiritual enemies that are invisible to our natural eyes. They are very cunning and utterly Hell-bent on destroying us. They are zealous in instigating us to do anything that would provoke God to anger
10. Because God cannot change, we must, or we will

never measure up to His standard. That requires sacrificial effort, so we need to pray for strength and focus.
11. The act of prayer demonstrates an understanding that the soul needs support or maintenance from its Creator. Failing to pray is like buying a new car and driving it without ever taking it for a tune-up or an oil change.
12. We pray not only against external attacks and temptations, but also for the strength to endure divine testing and the wisdom to understand our hearts' inclinations.
13. We pray because our knowledge is minimal, and we have minds like children compared to the boundless insight of those not restricted by the flesh such as the devil and the other fallen angels.
14. If praying is like a mini sacrifice to God because it requires time and discipline, fasting is the major one.
15. Fasting can produce results that significantly dwarf those realized by praying alone.

4

STEP 4 - WORSHIP AND DRAW CLOSER TO HIM

WEEK #4

CONFUSE THE ENEMY

The next time you start to worry.......

Begin to WORSHIP Instead!!

> By Him therefore **let us offer the sacrifice of praise to God continually**, that is, the fruit of our lips giving thanks to his name. (Hebrews 13:15 KJV)

Whoever offers praise glorifies Me, and to him who orders his conduct aright I will show the salvation of God. (Psalms 50:23, NKJV)

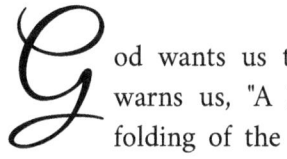od wants us to avoid poverty. Proverbs 24:33-34 warns us, "A little sleep, a little slumber, a little folding of the hands to rest, so shall your poverty

come like a prowler and your need like an armed man." Though those verses can also apply to physical needs, I believe the more urgent message pertains to spiritual impoverishment. Worship is a primary source of nourishment for the soul. We worship Him when we treat others fairly, serve Him through others, seek forgiveness, remain committed to repentance, study His Word, engage in godly thoughts and deeds, and stay on the narrow road.

THE PURPOSE OF WORSHIP

God inhabits the praises and worship of His people; He loves it when His creation adores Him and compliments Him. He is light, so our souls are enriched and revived with light, as it dissipates darkness, heals, and rejuvenates the soul. In Revelation 4:11, John wrote, "**For thou hast created all things, and for thy pleasure, they are and were created**." Pleasure is "a feeling of happy satisfaction and enjoyment," and satisfaction is "fulfillment of one's wishes, expectations, or the pleasure derived from it," according to the American English dictionary. Being fashioned in God's image has endowed humans with similar interests and desires, such as longing for acceptance. But if these desires are poorly managed, the result is a conflict of interest due to the soul's natural yearning to seek undeserved praise—all praises belong to God alone.

> *Therefore by Him let us continually offer the sacrifice of praise to God, that is, the fruit of our lips, giving thanks to His name. (Hebrews 13:15, NKJV)*

> *You alone are the Lord; You have made Heaven, The Heaven of heavens, with all their host, The Earth and everything on it, The seas and all that is in*

them, And You preserve them all. The host of Heaven worships You. (Nehemiah 9:6, NKJV)

REVERENCE IS DUE

Obtaining recognition for an achievement or going above and beyond expectation is admirable. As a loving Father and chief business owner—whose business entails managing His children's progress along the narrow way back to Heaven—God supports rewards systems. However, we have a natural propensity to capture recognition and hoard all the glory instead of forwarding them to the Sole Proprietor.

Neglecting to acknowledge God with thanksgiving is stealing His glory, and this is precisely what caused the expulsion of Lucifer from Heaven. Even today, that fallen, the monstrous creature is luring humans down the same path. The only way to arrest that decay of the soul is to repent. Go ahead and accept your reward but be sure to give Him thanks and do not revel in the deception that the achievement was an autonomous accomplishment. We can only do these things because Christ strengthens and allows us.

I can do all things through Christ who strengthens me. (Philippians 4:13, NKJV)

Give God the glory that He deserves because He created you. Show Him that you respect his involvement in your life. Every attainment is an opportunity for us to demonstrate our trustworthiness and thankfulness. Can God trust us with more? Management of God's allowance of gain is critical to the successful completion of the journey homeward.

He that is faithful in that which is least is faithful also

> *in much: and he that is unjust in the least is unjust also in much. (Luke 16:10, KJV)*

To worship God is to show devotion and demonstrate consecration, submission, attentiveness, and commitment. Worship is paying divine honor, giving reverence, and expressing respect. When we don't honor God in this manner, we are neither respecting Him nor giving Him the reverence or admiration He is owed. Who are you worshiping? If it is not God, you may be guilty of idolatry—worshiping an idol or false god.

Worship not intended for God is blasphemy, an expression of disrespect, and an act of stealing from God. Disobedience is the broad road to blasphemy against our loving Father. We can only effectively worship and love Him through obedience. Otherwise, the effort is a lie—an exercise in futility. We worship either God or the devil, and anyone who is living in rebellion does not worship God. Because we have been given free will, each soul can worship self, another person or thing, or God Himself. But why worship something or someone that is incomplete, fallen, imperfect, and needs help itself?

> *This people draweth nigh unto me with their mouth, and honoureth me with their lips, **but their heart is far from me**. But in vain they do worship me, teaching for doctrines the commandments of men. (Matthew 15:8-9, KJV)*

King Nebuchadnezzar's story is memorable because it demonstrates how serious an offense it is to divert worship away from the only wise and eternal God. The king became pompous enough to claim that "by his might and power," he had built the Babylonian empire.

> *The king spake, and said, is not this great Babylon, that I have built for the house of the kingdom by the might of my power, and for the honor of my majesty? KJV)*

But God was so upset with him that the arrogant King did not even get the chance to complete his thoughts. God dethroned him that very moment and banished him from civilization, so he was forced to live like an animal.

> *While the word was in the king's mouth, there fell a voice from Heaven, saying, O king Nebuchadnezzar, to thee it is spoken;* ***The kingdom is departed from thee****. (Daniel 4:30-31)*

> *The same hour was the thing fulfilled upon Nebuchadnezzar, and he was driven from men, and did eat grass as oxen, and his body was wet with the dew of Heaven, till his hairs were grown like eagles' feathers, and his nails like birds' claws. (Daniel 4:33, KJV)*

Today, there are many like Nebuchadnezzar in the world. They may not be a king ruling a nation, but perhaps they are an office manager, a guardian, or a pastor. Perhaps they are merely another unrepentant soul. In any case, they are all obstructing praises from ascending heavenward and worshiping themselves instead. Eternal ruin approaches unless they run into the arms of forgiveness and repentance.

MORE THAN DRAMA

Worshiping God is not limited to singing songs, dancing around, and raising hands joyfully in a church meeting. Yes, one can easily join in that kind of celebration when life is satisfactory, and there are more than pennies in the bank account. But true worship transcends emotion and self-satisfaction because it is rooted in truth, faith, and compliance. When we are grounded in truth, we can offer sacrifices of praise and worship, and this sets the stage for spiritual growth, keeps us on the narrow path, and gladdens God's heart. Overall, we worship Him with our voice and mind. We worship God with pleasant thoughts and righteous deeds, and our obedience leads the devotion.

> *And Jesus answered and said unto him, Get thee behind me, Satan, for it is written, **thou shalt worship the Lord thy God, and Him only shalt thou serve.** (Luke 4:8, KJV)*

> *O come, let us worship and bow down: **let us kneel before the LORD our maker.** For He is our God; and we are the people of his pasture, and the sheep of his hand. **Today if ye will hear his voice, Harden not your heart,** as in the provocation, and as in the day of temptation in the wilderness. (Psalms 95:6-8, KJV)*

> *And above all these things put on **charity**, which is the bond of perfectness. And let the **peace of God rule in your hearts [trust Him]**, to the which also ye are called in one body; and **be ye thankful.** Let the word of Christ dwell in you richly in all wisdom; **teaching and admonishing one another in psalms and hymns and spiritual songs, singing with grace in your hearts to the Lord.** And whatsoever ye do in word or deed, do all in the name of the Lord*

> *Jesus, **giving thanks to God and the Father** by him. (Colossians 3:14-17, KJV)*
>
> ***Sing unto the LORD, for He hath done excellent things:** this is known in all the Earth. (Isaiah 12:5, KJV)*
>
> *Exalt ye the LORD our God, and **worship at his footstool,** for He is holy. (Psalms 99:5, KJV)*

A PRIVILEGE AND A BLESSING

It is a privilege to talk with God, to praise Him, and to worship Him. This opportunity is a part of the free will package that expires upon one's final breath. After that, the freedom and convenience to worship Him are no longer applicable, particularly for those who fail to get back home. We need to appreciate His love and majesty and recognize how tiny and frail we are compared to His infiniteness.

> *No, for all the peoples of the world are nothing in comparison with him—they are but a drop in the bucket, dust on the scales. He picks up the islands as though they had no weight at all. (Isaiah 40:15, TLB)*

Yes, God accepts our praise and worship, but He does not need it; He is all-sufficient. Compared to our Creator, we are like miniaturized components on a large computer circuit board, spanning the landmass of this planet that Carl Sagan called the "pale blue dot." Can you exist without Him? I cannot. We are like grasshoppers before Him.

> *Canst thou make Him afraid as a grasshopper? the glory of His nostrils is terrible. (Job 39:20, KJV)*

> **He made the world and everything in it, and since he is Lord of heaven and earth, he doesn't live in man-made temples; and human hands can't minister to his needs—for he has no needs!** *He himself gives life and breath to everything, and satisfies every need there is. He created all the people of the world from one man, Adam, and scattered the nations across the face of the earth. He decided beforehand which should rise and fall, and when. He determined their boundaries. His purpose in all of this is that they should seek after God, and perhaps feel their way toward him and find him—though he is not far from any one of us.* **For in him we live and move and are!** *As one of your own poets says it, 'We are the sons of God. (Acts 17:24-28, TLB)*

We must respect that God is impressively awesome and terrifyingly righteous. Keep in mind that Satan is not in Hell because he can do any better, nor because he wants to be there, but because God's righteousness demands it. And no human can fully understand God because to do so would also mean having a full comprehension of infinity. No one has that capability. God's awesomeness should inspire us to worship Him.

Like the act of prayer, spending deliberate time in worship illuminates the soul, making it glow with health. The Israelites witnessed when Moses descended Mount Sinai with the Ten Commandments after spending 40 days with God.

> *And it came to pass, when Moses came down from mount Sinai with the two tables of testimony in*

> Moses' hand, when he came down from the mount,
> that Moses wist not that the skin of **his face shone
> while he talked with Him.** (Exodus 34:29, KJV)

In conclusion, a person worships God or self. The devil or another thing or being or person is only an incidental third-party recipient. We must be attentive and realize that the soul is the gatekeeper who decides whether to use an occasion to offer praise to God or hoard it and fatten itself with lies or pride.

Just as in the Garden of Eden, God is still guiding and commanding us with the same type of instructions He gave Eve. "**Do not touch this or that.**" "**Do not think about this or that.**" "**Do not say this or that.**" We decide whether to follow His voice or allow our hearts to pursue the lust of the eyes, flesh, and the pride of life.

Not worshiping God brings us to the story of the prodigal son, who squandered his inheritance on his desires. Neglecting to worship God is equivalent to lavishing ourselves with God's investment of life and time instead of using it to promote or advance His kingdom, and wasteful and unrepentant souls go to Hell.

> *Go to the ant, thou sluggard; consider her ways, and
> be wise.* (Proverbs 6:6, KJV)

True worship of God is reflected in a life of obedience. It is worshiping God in spirit and truth, not getting caught up in pride or self-promotion.

> ***O come, let us worship and bow down.*** *Let us kneel
> before the LORD our maker. For He is our God;
> and we are the people of his pasture, and the sheep
> of his hand. To day if ye will hear his voice, Harden
> not your heart, as in the provocation, and as in the*

day of temptation in the wilderness: When your fathers tempted me, proved me, and saw my work. (Psalms 95:6-9, KJV)

Sing unto the Lord; for He hath done excellent things; *this is known in all the Earth.* (Isaiah 12:5, KJV)

It is a good thing to give thanks unto the LORD, *and to sing praises unto thy name, O most High.* (Psalms 92:1, KJV)

Then saith Jesus unto him, get thee hence, Satan, for it is written, **thou shalt <u>worship</u> the Lord thy God, and Him only shalt thou <u>serve</u>.** *(Matthew 4:10, KJV)*

VERSES ABOUT WORSHIP

1. Oh come, let us sing to the Lord! Let us shout joyfully to the Rock of our salvation. Let us come before His presence with thanksgiving; Let us shout joyfully to Him with psalms. For the Lord is the great God, And the great King above all gods. (Psalms 95:1-3, NKJV)
2. Therefore, since we are receiving a kingdom which cannot be shaken, let us have grace, by which we may serve God acceptably with reverence and godly fear. (Hebrews 12:28, NKJV)
3. O worship the Lord in the beauty of holiness: fear before him, all the Earth. (Psalms 96:9, KJV)

DO THIS TODAY AND MAKE IT A LIFESTYLE

1. Worship God through kindness to others—be courteous and gentle in thought and speech.
2. Remember the challenges and pains He has brought you through. Tell Him thanks in songs, poetry, or personal melody.
3. Be thoughtful and thankful about Heaven and use this opportunity to get back there.
4. Tell Jesus thanks for dying for you and all the blessings in your life. Purpose yourself to be a thanks-giver, not a murmurer or complainer.

SUMMARY POINTS

1. To worship God is to show Him devotion, to demonstrate consecration, submission, attentiveness, and commitment. Worship is paying divine honor, giving reverence, and expressing respect.
2. Worship is a primary source of nourishment for the soul. We worship God when we treat others fairly, serve Him through serving others, seek forgiveness, remain committed to repentance, study His Word, engage in godly thoughts and deeds, and stay on the narrow road.
3. Neglecting to acknowledge God with thanksgiving is stealing His glory, which is precisely what caused the expulsion of Lucifer from Heaven.
4. We can accept rewards, but we must also thank Him. We should not revel in the deception that our achievement was a self-sufficient accomplishment.
5. Give God the pleasure and glory that He deserves because He created you. Show Him that you respect His involvement in your life. Every attainment is an opportunity for us to demonstrate our trustworthiness. Can God trust us with more?
6. Who are you worshiping? If it is not God, you may be guilty of idolatry, worshiping an idol or false god.
7. We can only effectively worship and love God through obedience. Otherwise, the effort is a lie—an exercise in futility.
8. We worship either God or the devil, and anyone who is living in rebellion is not worshiping God.
9. Because we have been given free will, each soul is enabled to worship self, another person or thing, or God Himself. But why worship something or

someone that is incomplete, fallen, imperfect, and needs help itself?
10. Worshiping God should not be limited to singing songs, dancing around, and raising hands joyfully in a church meeting. True worship transcends emotion and self-satisfaction because it is rooted in truth, faith, obedience, and a sacrificial lifestyle.
11. No human can fully understand God because to do so would also mean having a full comprehension of infinity or eternity. No one has that capability, so God's awesomeness should inspire us to worship Him.
12. Not worshiping God reminds us of the prodigal son's story, who squandered his inheritance.

5

STEP 5 - SERVE AND YOU WILL BE SERVED

WEEK #5

For, brethren, ye have been called unto liberty; only use not liberty for an occasion to the flesh, but **by love serve one another**. (Galatians 5:14 KJV)

Serve the LORD with gladness; Come before His presence with singing. Know that the LORD, He is God; It is He who has made us, and not we ourselves; We are His people and the sheep of His pasture. Enter into His gates with thanksgiving, And into His courts with praise. Be thankful to Him, and bless His name. (Psalms 100:2-4, NKJV)

*L*ike fish in a holding tank at a restaurant waiting to be served to the next patron, humans are busy swimming through life and time until either eternal life or death consumes them. However, unlike fish, we can select whose digestive system we want to serve, the divine or demonic. Now is the time to decide.

> *Let no man seek his own, but every man another's wealth.* (1 Corinthians 10:24, KJV)

THE NATURE OF A SERVICE

> *For God is not unjust; He will not forget your work and the love you demonstrated for his name by serving the saints—and by continuing to serve them.* (Hebrews 6:10, CSB)

We are served every day in ways that are not too easily recognizable. We turn on our computer, and behind the scenes, run millions of programmer lines that have been prepackaged by a programmer into small chunks and tagged with unique identifiers, which become unique functions or procedures. The only purpose is to serve the user as streams of commands flow in from the keyboard, mouse, or touchscreen and then produce a result. The combination of thousands of requests for services by human and interacting components is called a computer system.

This example is a microcosm of a more extraordinary interplay of God and His human creation, which, in my view, is appropriately described as art and science imitating life. PC components seamlessly interoperate using a common interface language. Similarly, love is the language or accepted protocol for efficient and profitable communication spanning Heaven and Earth. Love is the element that maintains unity in the body of Christ; it is foundational to obedience, to serving God and others. Love is God, and God is love, and we need love to serve or help as God does.

> *And now abide faith, hope, love, these three, but **the greatest of these is love**. (1 Corinthians 13:13, NKJV)*

> *Jesus said unto him, **thou shalt love the Lord thy God with all thy heart, and with all thy soul, and with all thy mind**. This is the first and great commandment. And the second is like unto it, **thou shalt love thy neighbor as thyself**. (Matthew 22:37-39, KJV)*

> *But above all these things **put on love, which is the bond of perfection**. (Colossians 3:14, NKJV)*

The concept of a computer with multiple subsystems, each performing a different role, is analogous to how the human body works. Hands perform different tasks than the feet do. On a broader scale, each of the more than 7 billion people worldwide is like a body part or computer procedure; each plays a role and serves the larger systems to be profitable or useful. The entire human experience is a huge theatrical performance in which actors interact and serve each other as the activity—the world—waltzes to a conclusion. These examples illustrate God's plan for his body, the group of earthlings who will reenter Heaven. He served us with His life, and He requires that we be of service to Him and others. To serve effectively and profitably is to perceive everything as being done unto the Lord, both in thoughts and deeds.

> *Let every soul be subject unto the higher powers.* ***For there is no power but of God; the powers that be are ordained of God.*** *(Romans 13:1, KJV)*

> *Servants, obey in all things your masters according to the flesh; not with eye-service, as men pleasers; but in singleness of heart, fearing God, and* ***whatsoever ye do, do it heartily, as to the Lord, and not unto men;*** *Knowing that of the Lord ye shall receive the reward of the inheritance: for ye serve the Lord Christ.* *(Colossians 3:22-24, KJV)*

Everyone is a member of a network of connectivity and interplay. We belong to the body of Christ, each member having a role no different than the functional relationship a branch has with a tree. God wants each person to have an elevated consciousness about the equality of each sibling or branch. We can pray for the ability to see this difficult truth.

Over time, I have learned that I need to pause and be thoughtful when serving others with a response to a question. I am learning to remove myself, focus on the person first, and then consider the request. I learned this approach by interacting with a needy person for years. At times, his requests for help were burdensome. Even if I told him that I did not have the funds to assist, he would find some other reason to keep coming, constantly jabbing my sensibility, patience, and even abuse my fear of the Lord. Still, I had to remember to respond as God would and offer a selfless response—responding respectfully and not venting frustration. The Bible says anger rests in the bosom of fools, and I don't want to be foolish. Foolishness—lack of good sense or judgment—is a sin.

> ***For from within, out of the heart of men,*** *proceed evil thoughts, adulteries, fornications, murders, Thefts,*

> *covetousness, wickedness, deceit, lasciviousness, an evil eye, blasphemy, pride, **foolishness:** all these evil things come from within, and defile the man. (Mark 7:21-23, KJV)*

> ***He that is slow to wrath is of great understanding,** but he that is hasty of spirit exalteth folly. (Proverbs 14:29, KJV)*

> *Be not hasty in thy spirit to be angry, for **anger resteth in the bosom of fools.** (Ecclesiastes 7:9, KJV)*

SERVING GOD THROUGH OTHERS

Regardless of others' perception, each life is equally as significant as all those who came before it, will come after it, and are its contemporaries. The optics of human vision cannot discover a person's value because God is invisible, and He has created each of His images, each soul, with that same hidden attribute. Each person is a version of Jesus. Whatever is done to any individual, the same is done to Jesus. Be careful about how you treat your Savior.

> *And the King shall answer and say unto them, verily I say unto you, **Inasmuch as ye have done it unto one of the least of these my brethren, ye have done it unto Me.** (Matthew 25:40, KJV)*

> ***If someone says, "I love God," and hates his brother, he is a liar,** for he who does not love his brother whom he has seen, **how can he love God whom he has not seen?** (1 John 4:20, NKJV)*

> *For God is not unrighteous to forget your work and*

> labor of love, which ye have shewed toward his
> name, in that ye have ministered to the saints, and
> do minister. (Hebrews 6:10, KJV)

Often, we do not recognize Jesus in others because of our fleshly desires, short-sightedness, and pride. We skip over Jesus as He begs for some change to buy food. We ignore Him as He seeks assistance to avoid eviction. We don't visit Him in jail or prison. We shun Him in His homelessness, and we curse Him over a customer service phone call. We berate Him at the workplace and don't give Him the raise or promotion He deserves. Yet, we want to enter His kingdom. Meanwhile, all He wants is to be treated fairly. He deserves to be served.

> Verily, verily, I say unto you, **the servant is not greater than his lord [Jesus served, so should we]**; neither He that is sent greater than he that sent him. (John 13:16, KJV)

> For even the Son of man came not to be ministered unto, but to minister [**serve**], and to give [**offer service**] his life a ransom for many. (Mark 10:45, KJV)

> And whatsoever ye do, **do it heartily, as to the Lord, and not unto men;** knowing that of the Lord ye shall receive the reward of the inheritance, for ye serve the Lord Christ. (Colossians 3:23-24, KJV)

> We serve other because **there is one body, and one Spirit,** even as ye are called in one hope of your calling; **One Lord, one faith, one baptism, One God and Father of all, who is above all, and through all, and in you all.** (Ephesians 4:4-6, KJV)

How do we set up the stage of our heart for serving God and others? Humility is the foundation. We must understand that God lives in each person in two ways: 1) He is the person's life, and 2) the soul is His image. The fleshly member is from the Earth and will eventually return to it. Therefore, excluding the physical body, we are spiritual beings from Heaven, where only love, unity, and humbleness exist.

In too many cases on Earth, we treat others like foreigners or aliens. This is very displeasing to God. Souls end up in Hell because of ill-treating Jesus through others, forgetting that it's God's own image that feels the pain of mistreatment. When we don't serve others, it causes a disconnection in the body of Christ.

Sir Richard Branson, an English business magnate, investor, author, and philanthropist, has described some qualities that I believe are emblematic of the types of qualities God desires of His people. Branson said, "To be successful, you must hit the ground running." Though he may be referring to secular business practices, I believe the same can be said for evangelism and for performing kindness to anyone, not only those with an ulterior motive. On the point of good customer service, Jesus, the CEO, epitomizes this quality.

> **Respect is how to treat everyone**, not just those you want to impress.
> *Courage is what it takes to stand up and speak;* **courage is also what it takes to sit down and listen.**
> **I have always believed that the way you treat your employees is the way they will treat your customers**, and that people flourish when they are praised.
> **To be successful,** you have to be out there, and **you have to hit the ground running.**

Good customer service begins at the top. If your senior people don't get it, even the strongest links further down the line can become compromised.

— SIR RICHARD BRANSON

The following is the list of ways we can serve others:

1. Think before you respond to a question to ensure against releasing a condescending tone, word, or expression.
2. Try to realize that you are speaking not only to the physical person but also to the person's soul and the Spirit of God who lives in the person. All are interacting with you. Therefore, show patience, kindness, compassion, hospitality, tolerance, gentleness, understanding, generosity, courtesy, and pleasantness to God, Jesus, and the Spirit. This is an example of the consequence or cascading effect of our actions and responses to others.
3. We serve others by praying for them. We petition for protection from physical and spiritual harm. We pray for power and consistency in obedience and a thorough understanding and acceptance of sin's consequences. We pray that they would recognize the enemy and appreciate the true friend, Jesus. We pray for patience and understanding of free will, and we pray for wisdom and strength to complete God's plan for them on Earth.
4. We serve others by helping them not to sin. Abstaining from fornication, homosexuality, adultery, lying, stealing, backbiting, and gossiping help ourselves and our brothers and sisters, which pleases God very much, and He will reward us accordingly.

5. Pray for the understanding that when we don't serve God, we obstruct His plans on Earth, and there is an eternal punishment for doing so unless forgiveness and repentance are sought. We cannot just decide to opt-out of serving God and others without consequences. He owns us. The belief that we own ourselves is a lie; the truth is we don't own anything. We are slaves to sin until we accept Jesus as our Lord and savior. (Galatians 4:7) If we are stiff-necked, with hearts hardened against Him, and opt for our way, then that is what we get, but the journey will not lead us heavenward.
6. We become better servants when we are filled with and led by the Holy Spirit (or Holy Ghost), as we read in Acts 4:31-37, Acts 5:1-6, and Acts 5:32.

For ye are bought with a price: therefore, glorify God in your body, and in your spirit, which are God's. (1 Corinthians 6:20, KJV)

Therefore you are no longer a slave but a son, and if a son, then an heir of God through Christ. (Galatians 4:7, NKJV)

"And when they had prayed, the place was shaken where they were assembled together; and they were all filled with the **Holy Ghost**, and they spake the word of God with boldness. And the multitude of them that believed were of one heart and of one soul; neither said any of them that ought of the things which he possessed was his own; but they had all things common. And with great power gave the apostles witness of the resurrection of the Lord Jesus and great grace was upon them all. Neither was *there any among them that lacked, for as many as were possessors of lands or houses sold them, and brought the prices of the things that were sold, and laid them down at the apostles' feet: and distribution was made unto every man according as he had need. And Joses, who by the apostles was surnamed Barnabas, (which is, being interpreted, The son of consolation,) a Levite, and of the country of Cyprus, having land, sold it, and brought the money, and laid it at the apostles' feet. (Acts 4:31-37)*

But a certain man named Ananias, with Sapphira his wife, sold a possession, And kept back part of the price, his wife also being privy to it, and brought a certain part, and laid it at the apostles' feet. But Peter said, Ananias, why hath **Satan filled thine heart to lie to the Holy Ghost***, and to keep back part of the price of the land? Whiles it remained, was it not thine own? and after it was sold, was it not in thine own power? why hast thou conceived this thing in thine heart? thou hast not lied unto men, but unto God. And Ananias hearing these words fell down, and gave up the ghost: and great fear came on all them that heard these things. And the young men arose, wound him up, and carried him out, and buried him. (Acts 5:1-6, KJV)*

And we are his witnesses of these things [the miracles]; and so is also the Holy Ghost, **whom God hath given to them that <u>obey</u> Him** *[disobedience is darkness and the Holy Ghost is light]. (Acts 5:32, KJV)*

Ye stiff-necked [arrogant and stubborn] and

> *uncircumcised in heart and ears,* **ye do always resist the Holy Ghost**, *as your fathers did, so do ye. (Acts 7:51, KJV)*

A GENEROUS COMPENSATION

Jesus is the most generous employer. When He created the world, He instituted a just and equitable compensation system. For example, the Israelites benefitted from reparations during their exodus from slavery in Egypt. The same compensatory practices help each soul as it labors to its heart's content. There are only two types of wages: one is eternal life, and the other is eternal death. This is full payment for the kind and quality of work the soul does on Earth. Serving others is a compensated undertaking. We may give a poor person money or offer to carry a heavy basket or bag for the elderly, and for that, we will be compensated. But we also help them and honor God simply by thinking kindly about them. Perhaps surprising, earnings are also distributed for sinful activities—but these are the wages of death. Payments are assessed for both thoughts and deeds. Even thinking is labor because it uses God-given energy. Therefore, we shouldn't backbite or gossip about anyone. Instead, we should always pray for the very best for them. God smiles with delight when we serve others.

> ***For the wages of sin is death**, but the gift of God is eternal life in Christ Jesus our Lord. (Romans 6:23, NKJV)*

> ***He that hath pity upon the poor lendeth unto the Lord**, and that which he hath given will He pay him again. (Proverbs 19:17, KJV)*

> ***Give to him who asks you**, and from him who wants*

to borrow from you do not turn away. (Matthew 5:42, NKJV)

Just as Heaven serves humanity, Hell attempts to do the same. Satan and other demons can transform themselves into angels of light to lure us into destructive situations. The strategy against such a possibility is to strive to be holy by pursuing forgiveness, repentance, prayer, and worship—in short, by putting on the whole armor of God.

> *And no wonder!* ***For Satan himself transforms himself into an angel of light.*** *(2 Corinthians 11:14, NKJV)*

> *Finally, my brethren,* ***be strong in the Lord and in the power of His might. Put on the whole armor of God****, that you may be able to stand against the wiles of the devil. (Ephesians 6:10-11, NKJV)*

> ***For God is not unjust to forget your work and labor of love which you have shown toward His name****, in that you have ministered to the saints, and do minister. (Hebrews 6:10, NKJV)*

VERSES ABOUT SERVICE

1. I beseech you therefore, brethren, by the mercies of God, that ye present [offer, serve] your bodies a living sacrifice, holy, acceptable unto God, which is your reasonable service. (Romans 12:1, KJV)
2. For even the Son of Man [Jesus] did not come to be served, but to serve, and to give His life a ransom for many. (Mark 10:45, NKJV)

3. Let nothing be done through strife or vainglory; but in lowliness of mind let each esteem other better than themselves. (Philippians 2:3, KJV)

DO THIS TODAY AND MAKE IT A LIFESTYLE

1. Pray for your families, friends, and others to overcome the world by the Blood of the Lamb and reenter Heaven.
2. Be generous—share money, food, clothing, smiles, and pleasant thoughts—reject backbiting and gossip.
3. Serve God with obedience, which leads to holiness.
4. Pursue fasting for God's will to be done on Earth as it is done in Heaven.

SUMMARY POINTS

1. How do we set up the stage of our heart to serve God and others? Humility is the foundation. We must understand that God lives in each person in two ways: He is the person's life, and the soul is His image.
2. Each person is a version of Jesus. Whatever is done to any individual, the same is done to Jesus. Be careful about how you treat your Savior—indirectly.
3. Jesus served us and others with His life, and He requires that we be of service to Him and others.
4. We become better servants when we are filled with and led by the Holy Spirit (or Holy Ghost), as we read in Acts 4:31-37, Acts 5:1-6, and Acts 5:32.
5. The entire human experience is a theatrical performance in which actors interact and serve each other as the activity—the world—waltzes to a conclusion.
6. Love is the element that maintains unity in the body of Christ; it is foundational to obedience, to serving God and others. Love is God, and God is love, and we need love to serve or help as God does.
7. Jesus tells us that a servant is not greater than his master. Because we are servants, we must accept that responsibility, even to the extent of enduring hardship and persecution for Jesus' sake.
8. Think before responding to a question to ensure against releasing a condescending tone, word, or expression.
9. We serve others by praying for them. We petition for protection from physical and spiritual harm on their behalf.
10. We serve others by helping them not to sin.

Abstaining from fornication, homosexuality, adultery, lying, stealing, backbiting, gossiping, and immorality helps not only ourselves but also our brothers and sisters.

11. Serving others is a compensated undertaking. We may give a poor person money or offer to carry a heavy basket or bag for the elderly. We also help them and honor God when we think kindly about them.

STEP 6 - STUDY AND SHOW YOURSELF APPROVED

WEEK #6

STUDY
THE BIBLE

> Habitual sins will distance you from the Bible, owing to guilt and a deceptive feeling of condemnation. Reading and believing the Bible will keep you from sin and condemnation.

He answered, It is written: Man must not live on bread alone but on every word that comes from the mouth of God. (Matthew 4:4, CSB)

Life is a test designed by God. Considering that He likes to keep things level because we are children, there is only one textbook—the Bible. With its assortment of experiences, life on Earth is like a college curriculum that consists of two subjects, obedience and disobedience. Within those two subjects is an array of accountability, natural and spiritual laws for human interaction, protocol and etiquette for divine communication, stewardship, ambassadorship, and strategies against compromise, complacency, and procrastination. If we fail to read the required material, the only grade we should expect is an F. Fallen angels are good-for-nothing former students who miserably have failed while they were in Heaven. Now they prowl around on our spiritual campus, cunningly and persistently trying to create idlers out of us. Part of the test that faces us is to analyze and classify information so we can identify the campus loiterers, avoid them, and avoid the extracurricular activity known as sin.

> *Be sober, be vigilant; because your adversary the devil, as a roaring lion, walketh about, seeking whom he may devour.* (1 Peter 5:8, KJV)

TYPES OF INFORMATION

There are two types of information we absorb, spiritual and secular. Spiritual information is a discovery about the invisible world, while secular information explains the visible or natural realm. An entire lifetime can be spent addressing the knowledge deficits we have about these subjects. It's a personal decision, courtesy of our free will, but it is not without an opportunity cost. The scope and value of accumulated details are constrained by time, and either wisdom or foolhardiness governs the efforts. Have you ever heard the proverb, "All work and no play makes Jack a dull boy?" "Catering only for the secular leaves no room for the spiritual" is a sobering expression that describes an intrinsically spiritual life that invests exclusively in temporary matters.

Many of us have accumulated a treasury of temporal knowledge from years in school and college, workplace experiences, and personal interactions. During those information-gathering years, a mission-focused mindset was essential because results determined whether a prospective employer would be interested in hiring or not. Very few individuals assign much time to Bible-reading or spiritual knowledge. God has observed our inattentiveness to His Word with jealous eyes and a saddened heart. He wants us to repent before it is too late.

WHAT THE BIBLE TEACHES

We don't need Highly Superior Autobiographical Memory (HSAM) or King Solomon's wisdom to study the Bible. Discipline, a desire to understand oneself (spiritual and physical), a willingness to prepare for life beyond the grave, and a respect for God are sufficient factors.

> *Highly Superior Autobiographical Memory (HSAM) is characterized as the ability to accurately recall an exceptional number of experiences and their associated dates from events occurring throughout much of one's lifetime.*
>
> — WWW.NCBI.NLM.NIH.GOV

In the Bible, we find vitally important information:

1. No one disappears at death. Life continues forever in Heaven or Hell, so forget about "*We therefore commit this body to the ground, Earth to Earth, ashes to ashes, dust to dust; in sure, and certain hope of the Resurrection to eternal life*," especially if the deceased never accepted Christ as Lord—there is no eternal life outside of Him.
2. Everything we see was first designed or considered in eternity because we are made in the likeness of the invisible God, who is from eternity. Our souls reside

in the eternal realm, even while our physical bodies are on Earth. Jesus is the first created being, and God created the world through Him and for Him.
3. God is love, but He does not hesitate to punish evildoers. He will give wages for both good and evil because decisions and efforts are spent to commit them.
4. We do not own ourselves. We will give Him an account of how we use life and time on Earth.
5. The servant is not greater than the master. Jesus suffered, and so will we. We must brace ourselves for impact.
6. Jesus loves us so much that He surrendered His majesty and died on a cross as payment for us to get back to Heaven.
7. God cannot change owing to His perfection. We can wholeheartedly trust Him, but we cannot place any time restriction on Him. He controls both us and time. He does not need to repent because He is the same yesterday, today, and forever. He does no wrong, so there is no need to change.
8. Though God loves and wants the best for us, He still wants us to ask Him for help. It is a spiritual principle. If we lack something that we need, it is because we haven't asked for it. The Bible tells us to ask so that our joy may be full.

> ***Ask, and it shall be given you; seek, and ye shall find; knock, and it shall be opened unto you,*** *For every one that asketh receiveth; and he that seeketh findeth; and to him that knocketh it shall be opened. (Matthew 7:7-8, KJV)*

> *Ye lust, and have not: ye kill, and desire to have, and*

> cannot obtain: ye fight and war, **yet ye have not, because ye ask not.** *(James 4:2, KJV)*

> Hitherto have ye asked nothing in my name: **ask, and ye shall receive, that your joy may be full.** *(John 16:24, KJV)*

> **My covenant will I not break,** nor alter the thing that is gone out of my lips. *(Psalms 89:34, KJV)*

> **God is not a man, that He should lie; neither the son of man, that He should repent:** hath He said, and shall He not do it? or hath He spoken, and shall He not make it good? *(Numbers 23:19, KJV)*

> Remember the word that I said unto you, **the servant is not greater than his lord.** *(John 15:20, KJV)*

A TACTICAL GUIDE

> This Book of the Law shall not depart from your mouth, but you shall meditate in it day and night, that you may observe to do according to all that is written in it. For then you will make your way prosperous, and then you will have good success. *(Joshua 1:8, NKJV)*

Now, why should we study the manual that God Himself inspired mortal men to write? We learn about ourselves, our Creator and Friend, and the enemy. We also learn about our past, our present, and our future. The Bible is not only the roadmap to show us how to get back home to Heaven, but it is also a survival guide to avoid any pitfalls during the journey.

Perils are not only external but also internal. For example, life and death are in the power of the tongue; our Creator is angry with the wicked every day, and souls don't go to Hell merely for doing wrong, but because they fail to repent and live in a holy manner until they leave the Earth.

The Scripture teaches that the Word is God. The Bible is a living book. The messages it contains are not ordinary text. They are eternal in cause and effect, but we often treat them recklessly and disregard what they convey. Communications that offer secular results are the kind of words we tend to quickly act upon or take seriously, especially those that produce the type of impact that threatens our comfort or livelihood. Other words are brushed aside or placed in the complacency bin. God's commands rank highest on the list of disregarded, instruction-oriented words. The Bible is the Book of books, approved by our Creator, representing the Father as He speaks to His children. We are the product of words spoken in creation because the Word existed before us, and God is the Word.

> *In the beginning was the Word, and the Word was with God, and the Word was God. (John 1:1, KJV)*

> *And* ***the Word was made flesh, and dwelt among us****, (and we beheld his glory, the glory as of the only begotten of the Father,) full of grace and truth. (John 1:14, KJV)*

> *But He answered and said, it is written,* ***man shall not live by bread alone, but by every word that proceedeth out of the mouth of God****. (Matthew 4:4, KJV)*

On judgment day, the Lord will ask many why they did not read and study His Word, and some will say they were too busy or that they did not understand it. That response would be a lie for most, if not all, particularly for those who can read and are capable of buying a copy of the most bestselling book of all time. We find some interesting stats about Bible sales at thebibleanswer.org:

> *The Bible is by far the worlds best-selling book of all time. No other book, fact or fiction, even comes close. Most estimates place the number of Bibles printed each year at over 100 million. 20 million Bibles are sold each year in the United States alone.*
> 273,972 a day
> 11,415 an hour
> 190 a minute
> 3 a second
>
> — THEBIBLEANSWER.ORG

Many people have the mistaken belief that the Bible is merely a historical reference. It has chapters, page numbers, and various accounts of lives that have gone before us, much like any other book. A biology book describes living organisms. A physics text communicates what God has revealed to us about matter and energy. A math book addresses calculations or conclusions based on facts, figures, quantities, and shapes. But the Bible is a voice telling us we will soon depart from this world, so we need to prepare for departure to eternity.

> *But He answered and said, It is written,* **man shall not live by bread alone, but by every word that proceedeth out of the mouth of God.** *(Matthew 4:4, KJV)*

LIVE THE WORD BY FAITH

Still, some are challenged to accept the Word of God for two reasons. First, they question the source's authenticity because there is doubt about whether the writers actually heard from God. Second, they debate or even deny God's very existence. But 2 Timothy 3:16-17 reminds us God's inspiration gives all scripture. The Bible informs us that God is invisible, so the only option we have in receiving the Bible, as intentionally directed by God, is to embrace it by faith. We can only please Him by trusting Him. Exercising faith is applying effort to overcome doubt. God will compensate us with wages of life or death according to how we treat His Word. God says the just shall live by faith, and that requirement is not a foreign concept at all. For example, we breathe air with delight and confidence even though we cannot see it—we inhale by faith. We accept the concepts of truth and falsehood—although we cannot see them, we have faith that they exist in the spiritual world in a real way.

> *For therein is the righteousness of God revealed from faith to faith, as it is written,* **the just shall live by faith.** *(Romans 1:17, KJV)*

> **All scripture is given by inspiration of God,** *and is profitable for doctrine [policy, guideline], for reproof [scolding or chastisement, reprimand or rebuke formally], for correction, for instruction in righteousness: That the man of God may be perfect, throughly furnished unto all good works. (2 Timothy 3:16-17, KJV)*

We willingly accept the possibility of angels in the flesh though only a few have seen them. Somehow, I believe that in our innermost being, we know God exists and that the Bible is

His guide, but to accept that truth means we also accept the responsibility to live it out. Therein lies the conflict. Embracing the Bible means adapting to a new, God-fearing lifestyle, and perhaps many are not ready to make that commitment. They think, dangerously, that tomorrow is a better day to decide.

Still, we cannot ignore God and walk away scot-free. The divine system does not function in that manner; it does not allow for disobedience or disregard. Satan's primary strategy is to cause one to postpone accepting God at His Word until time runs out. Wisdom means ignoring demons and bracing for the unavoidable. We must become doers of the Word; if we don't, we will perish.

> ***But be ye doers of the word****, and not hearers/readers only, deceiving your own selves. For if any be a hearer of the word, and not a doer, he is like unto a man beholding his natural face in a glass, for he beholdeth himself, and goeth his way, and straightway forgetteth what manner of man he was. (James 1:22-24, KJV)*

> ***My people are destroyed for lack of knowledge****, because thou hast rejected knowledge, I will also reject thee, that thou shalt be no priest to me: seeing thou hast forgotten the law of thy God, I will also forget thy children. (Hosea 4:6, KJV)*

MORE THAN A HISTORY BOOK

The Bible is a multidimensional, divine script. It's not flat, and it's not of one scope or extent; if it were, it would be merely a lifeless history book. Instead, it is the primary book of dualities, forming the basis of free will and always presenting us with two options. Some of the more familiar dualities include combinations such as love/hate, joy/pain, profitable/unprofitable, godliness/ungodliness, truth/lie, and hidden/revealed. A significant duality, the blessings and curses model, is described in Deuteronomy 28. Read the entire chapter for more insight on how to remain on the narrow path—because sin will knock us off while holiness will maintain us.

> *And it shall come to pass, **if thou shalt hearken diligently unto the voice of the LORD thy God, to observe and to do all his commandments which I command thee this day**, that the LORD thy God will set thee on high above all nations of the Earth: And all these blessings shall come on thee, and overtake thee, if thou shalt hearken unto the voice of the LORD thy God. Blessed shalt thou be in the city, and blessed shalt thou be in the field. Blessed shall be the fruit of thy body, and the fruit of thy ground, and the fruit of thy cattle, the increase of thy kine [cow/cattle], and the flocks of thy sheep. Blessed shall be thy basket and thy store. Blessed shalt thou be when thou comest in, and blessed shalt thou be when thou goest out. (Deuteronomy 28:1-6, KJV)*

> *Ye shall make you no idols nor graven image, neither rear you up a standing image, neither shall ye set up any image of stone in your land, to bow down unto it: for I am the LORD your God. Ye shall keep my sabbaths, and reverence my sanctuary: I am the LORD. **If ye walk in my statutes, and keep my commandments, and do them;** Then I will give you rain in due season, and the land shall yield her increase, and the trees of the field shall yield their fruit. And your threshing shall reach unto the vintage, and the vintage shall reach unto the sowing*

time: and ye shall eat your bread to the full, and
dwell in your land safely. And I will give peace in
the land, and ye shall lie down, and none shall make
you afraid: and I will rid evil beasts out of the land,
neither shall the sword go through your land...
(Leviticus 26:1-6, KJV)

— THE BLESSINGS MODEL

**But it shall come to pass, if thou wilt not hearken
unto the voice of the LORD thy God, to observe to
do all his commandments and his statutes which
I command thee this day;** that all these curses shall
come upon thee, and overtake thee: Cursed shalt
thou be in the city, and cursed shalt thou be in the
field. Cursed shall be thy basket and thy store.
Cursed shall be the fruit of thy body, and the fruit
of thy land, the increase of thy kine, and the flocks
of thy sheep. Cursed shalt thou be when thou comest
in, and cursed shalt thou be when thou goest out.
(Deuteronomy 28:15-19, KJV)

**But if ye will not hearken unto me, and will not do
all these commandments; And if ye shall despise
my statutes, or if your soul abhor my
judgments, so that ye will not do all my
commandments, but that ye break my covenant:
I also will do this unto you;** I will even appoint
over you terror, consumption, and the burning
ague, that shall consume the eyes, and cause sorrow
of heart: and ye shall sow your seed in vain, for
your enemies shall eat it. And I will set my face
against you, and ye shall be slain before your
enemies: they that hate you shall reign over you;

> and ye shall flee when none pursueth you.
> (Leviticus 26:14-17, KJV)

> — THE CURSES MODEL

NUTRITIONAL MAINTENANCE

Our physical bodies lose billions of red blood cells every day, and they are replaced to a greater degree with proper nutrition. Similarly, a soul needs to be repaired as well because unrepentant sins corrode it. Reading and confessing the Word in the Bible, with faith, helps to arrest the corrosion and heal the soul.

> *For whatever things were written before were written for our learning, that we through the patience and comfort of the Scriptures might have hope. (Romans 15:4, NKJV)*

VERSES ABOUT STUDY

1. Study to shew thyself approved unto God, a workman that needeth not to be ashamed, rightly dividing the word of truth. (2 Timothy 2:15, KJV)
2. The heart of the prudent acquires knowledge, And the ear of the wise seeks knowledge. (Proverbs 18:15, NKJV)
3. Give instruction to a wise man, and he will be still wiser; teach a just man, and he will increase in learning. (Proverbs 9:9, NKJV)

DO THIS TODAY AND MAKE IT A LIFESTYLE

1. Dedicate at least 15-30 minutes a day to Bible reading.
2. Refer to Deuteronomy 28 as often as required to boost alertness to the reality that we in a world of blessings and curses.
3. Understand that knowledge of the Bible teaches us to pray effectively—we gain an awareness of what He likes and dislikes.

SUMMARY POINTS

1. There are two types of information we absorb, spiritual and secular. Spiritual information is a discovery about the invisible world, while secular information explains the visible or natural realm.
2. We don't need Highly Superior Autobiographical Memory (HSAM) or King Solomon's wisdom to study the Bible.
3. Why should we study the manual that God himself inspired mortal men to write? We learn about ourselves, our Creator and Friend, and the enemy. We also learn about our past, our present, and our future.
4. The Bible is not only the roadmap to show us how to get back home to Heaven, but it is also a survival guide to avoid any pitfalls during the journey.
5. The Bible is the Book of books, approved by our Creator, representing the Father as He speaks to His children.
6. On judgment day, the Lord will ask many why they did not read and study His Word, and some will say they were too busy or that they did not understand it. That response would be a lie for most.
7. The Bible is a voice telling us we'll soon depart from this world, so we need to prepare for departure to live forever—we never die but <u>live</u> in Heaven or Hell. The word "live" here indicates we have feeling and senses in Heaven and Hell.
8. The Bible informs us that God is invisible, so the only option we have in receiving the Bible, as intentionally directed by God, is to embrace it by faith.
9. Embracing the Bible means adapting to a new, God-fearing lifestyle, and perhaps many are not ready to

make that commitment. They think, dangerously, that tomorrow is a better day to decide.
10. Satan's primary tactic is to cause one to postpone accepting God at His Word until time runs out. Wisdom means ignoring demons and bracing for the unavoidable.
11. The Bible is a multidimensional, divine script. It's not flat, and it's not of one scope or extent; if it were, it would be merely a lifeless history book.
12. The Bible is the primary book of dualities and forms the basis of free will.

STEP 7 - SANCTIFY AND YOU WILL SEE GOD

WEEK #7

> Now may the God of peace Himself sanctify you completely, and may your whole spirit, soul, and body be preserved blameless at the coming of our Lord Jesus Christ. (1 Thessalonians 5:23 NKJV)

Abstain from every form of evil. Now may the God of peace Himself sanctify you completely; and may your whole spirit, soul, and body be preserved blameless at the coming of our Lord Jesus Christ. (1 Thessalonians 5:22-23, NKJV)

Living by the Spirit is doing what God says to do; He is the Spirit and the Word. Carnality is the opposite, living by the flesh or being driven by self-will. God hates carnality because it is destructive to His image, the soul. The solution is to pray without ceasing and give thanks in every situation to gain the strength to fight the good fight. Try to keep quiet except to offer praise and never grumble in challenging situations. What you say can and will be used against you by the accuser, Satan. Wherever you are today in life, God has allowed it by His divine justice and mercy, so accept it with a grateful heart and keep praying for His will to be done and for power to endure to the end.

UNDERSTANDING SANCTIFICATION

> ***Ye are the light of the world** [as representative of Jesus]. A city that is set on an hill cannot be hid. Neither do men light a candle, and put it under a bushel, but on a candlestick; and it giveth light unto all that are in the house. **Let your light so shine before men, that they may see your good works**, and glorify your Father which is in Heaven.*
> *(Matthew 5:14-16, KJV)*

Sanctification is the strategically focused and practical approach to becoming more and more like Jesus. It is well documented that God is intolerant of sin, passionate about morality, and consummate in holiness. His godliness requirement is so unquestionable, complete, and conclusive that the Bible sternly warns without holiness or purity, no person will see Him; no one will get back home if they are not holy. Holiness is indeed another word for perfection, and it is not possible for a fallen, imperfect being to ever become perfect—without Jesus.

Sanctification is simply the process of living an obedient life, day by day. It requires a basic understanding that, although failure is "expected," the correct attitude is one that consistently seeks to avoid it. A strong, heartfelt inclination to shun all wrongdoing is the mission statement for consecration and dedication on the journey back home. To better appreciate its meaning and application, recognize that the reason Lucifer became a fallen angel named Satan is also that which oversees the eternal destruction of a soul—disobedience. Disobedience leads to desecration and sin. We are each the manager of our own lives, and God expects us to conduct life profitably. Pursuing disobedience is a mismanagement of God-given resources.

> *Follow peace with all men, and holiness, **without which no man shall see the Lord**. (Hebrews 12:14, KJV)*

THE IMPACT OF HOLINESS

> *But know that the LORD has set apart for Himself him who is godly; The LORD will hear when I call to Him. (Psalms 4:3, NKJV)*

Holiness is the packaging that encompasses forgiveness, repentance, prayer, worship, service, and study. Steadfastness in these activities will ensure a safe trip heavenward because no one gets into Heaven without achieving perfection—not even those who lived before Jesus. Except for Enoch[1], who God translated or raptured away because of his faith, the righteous souls who predated the First Coming of Christ over 2,000 years ago were held in Abraham's bosom after death. In contrast, the others descended into the eternal ravine of Hell.

> ***Be ye therefore perfect**, even as your Father which is in Heaven is perfect. (Matthew 5:48, KJV)*

> *By faith **Enoch was translated that he should not see death**; and was not found, because God had translated him: for before his translation he had this testimony, that he pleased God. (Hebrews 11:5, KJV)*

> *And **it came to pass, that the beggar [Lazarus] died, and was carried by the angels into Abraham's bosom**. The rich man also died, and was buried; and in Hell he lift up his eyes, being in torments, and seeth Abraham afar off, and Lazarus in his bosom. (Luke 16:22-23, KJV)*

Why were the righteous held in Abraham's bosom rather than going straight into Heaven? They were righteous, but they still needed to be adorned in perfection, a provision that Jesus accomplished with His death on the cross. God's requirement for holiness is absolute. Before the advent of Christ, the ritualistic atonement for sin was accomplished using bulls and goats' blood. However, this type of sacrificial offering was insufficient to attain perfection because everything on Earth, from humans to beasts, is imperfect. Jesus became the divine offering, transforming the soul into perfection once and for all through salvation. No priest needs to make daily or yearly reparations ever again.

> *But in those sacrifices there is a remembrance again made of sins every year. **For it is not possible that the blood of bulls and of goats should take away sins**. (Hebrews 10:3-4, KJV)*

SPIRITUAL ADJUSTMENTS

The Earth is a place for spiritual adjustments and refinements; sanctification is the profitable management of life and time during this process. When a soul accepts God's pruning hand, it demonstrates its level of seriousness, commitment, and accountability. This type of relationship gladdens our Father's heart. Sanctity is the best life now; it is seated in heavenly places with Christ while still alive. If a soul were a battery, a sanctified soul would be fully charged with sufficient energy to fight the good fight, resist the devil, overcome temptation, and make it back home. However, sin discharges the battery, subjecting the soul to defeat and eternal uselessness if repentance (or recharging) is not sought promptly.

> *And **cast ye the unprofitable servant into outer darkness**; there shall be weeping and gnashing of teeth. (Matthew 25:30, KJV)*

> *Even when we were dead in sins, hath quickened us together with Christ, (by grace ye are saved;) And **hath raised us up together, and made us sit together in heavenly places in Christ Jesus**. (Ephesians 2:5-6, KJV)*

In the Sermon on the Mount, Jesus describes the elements that are found in a sanctified life.

> *Matthew 5:3-11 (KJV)*
> 3 *Blessed are the **poor in spirit**: for theirs is the kingdom of Heaven.*
> 4 *Blessed are they that **mourn**: for they shall be comforted.*
> 5 *Blessed are the **meek**: for they shall inherit the Earth.*
> 6 *Blessed are they which do **hunger and thirst after righteousness**: for they shall be filled.*

> 7 Blessed are the **merciful:** for they shall obtain mercy.
> 8 Blessed are the **pure in heart:** for they shall see God.
> 9 Blessed are the **peacemakers:** for they shall be called the children of God.
> 10 Blessed are they **which are persecuted for righteousness' sake:** for theirs is the kingdom of Heaven.
> 11 Blessed are ye, **when men shall revile you, and persecute you,** and shall say all manner of evil against you falsely, for my sake.
>
> — THE BEATITUDES - THE BLESSINGS LISTED BY JESUS IN THE SERMON ON THE MOUNT

A SANCTIFIED SOUL

Like any other spiritual characteristic, holiness begins in eternity because it resides in the heart—the soul—and never leaves the spiritual world. Thoughts and deeds originate in the soul, and holiness—or the lack thereof—reflects the heart. While it is true that people can think one way and act another, that condition specifically relates to deception, an ingredient of wickedness.

> *For as he thinketh in his heart, so is he;* eat and drink, saith he to thee; but his heart is not with thee. (Proverbs 23:7, KJV)

Joseph is an excellent example of someone who physically and spiritually ran from evil. He was committed to living righteously before God and man, even when Potiphar's wife tried to seduce him. Joseph's response was epic: "How then can I do this great wickedness [adultery] and sin against God?" Joseph's strong convictions demonstrated no-nonsense confidence in the sovereignty of Christ and the importance of obedience and holiness. In our modern society, because hearts are becoming eviler, we must think carefully about Heaven and Hell. We *must* consider our eternal future and live with the end in mind because the end will come to each of us, whether we are ready or not.

> *And it came to pass after these things, that his master's wife cast her eyes upon Joseph; and she said, Lie with me. But he refused, and said unto his master's wife, Behold, my master wotteth not what is with me in the house, and he hath committed all that he hath to my hand; there is none greater in this house than I; neither hath he kept back anything from me but thee, because thou art his wife:* **how then can I do this great wickedness, and sin against God?** *(Genesis 39:7-9, KJV)*

A SACRIFICED BODY

Just as the body consumes food, our physical bodies in a sacrificial, not a cannibalistic, way are (supposed to be) consumables for God. The type of sacrifice that God desires does not destroy the body or render it useless; instead, the body is transformed into a more hospitable temple. He wants us to offer Him our self-denial service, spiritual discipline, moderation, and spiritual soberness. This effort can be quite arduous, even painful, but it is the pathway to growing and maintaining holiness. It is true that when we fast or deny ourselves in some way, it is usually uncomfortable. Still, it pleases God because it is a reverential act of presenting oneself as a living sacrifice.

> *I beseech you therefore, brethren, by the mercies of God, that ye **present your bodies a living sacrifice [fasting, fleeing sins]**, holy, acceptable unto God, which is your reasonable service.* (Romans 12:1, KJV)

Maintaining a lifetime of holiness requires a long-term, persistent, and patient investment strategy of life and time so that one can yield a favorable return on Earth and in the hereafter. God will bless the upright on this planet as well, not only in Heaven. Still, we must be prepared to live sacrificially. We achieve this daily as we follow God and are committed to obedience, and when we invest our life and time effectively, God is a generous paymaster.

> *But without faith it is impossible to please him: for he that cometh to God must believe that He is, and that **He is a rewarder of them that diligently seek him**.* (Hebrews 11:6, KJV)

It is imperative to remember that the same three attacks that caused Adam and Eve to fall are ones we must overcome: the lust of the flesh, the lust of the eyes, and the pride of life. To live sacrificially is ultimately rewarding because it is a life that God approves. It's a search for the Truth. It's a wise approach to life. It's an effort to discard thoughts that promote lies. Most of all, it's an effort to get out of a dream state and face the realities of life and time, of living and dying, of Heaven and Hell, blessings and curses, to find a true friend in Christ and be able to recognize the enemy, Satan.

A LIFESTYLE OF HOLINESS

As one matures in holiness, it will be easier to maintain it. Holiness will become a way of life, not a constant struggle to maintain spiritual sobriety. That level of growth is achieved as one's free will decides for God more and more frequently. The spiritual expansion can reach a level that any sinful thought is driven from one's mind without even a second thought, much less developing into a completely unhealthy idea. Like Peter and other disciples, we can live in triumph, rejoicing to be found worthy to suffer for Christ.

> *And they departed from the presence of the council,* ***rejoicing that they were counted worthy to suffer shame [after being beaten] for his name.*** *(Acts 5:41, KJV)*

To willingly and happily endure punishment for witnessing is quite extraordinary. The reassurance of a great reward for such a sacrifice is only achievable by supernatural assistance beyond this life and time. The Holy Spirit is the divine Godhead member Who provides the strength and motivation that feeds an obedient, holy soul, thereby enabling the person to experience and demonstrate the fruits of the Spirit.

> *But the fruit of the Spirit is love, joy, peace, patience, kindness, goodness, faithfulness, gentleness, self-control; against such things there is no law. (Galatians 5:22-23, ESV)*

In his book *The Holy Spirit*, Billy Graham writes,

> "These fruits are like clusters of grapes.

> *The **first cluster** of the **fruit**, Love, Joy and Peace, has a primary Godward relationship, with outward results that others can see. Thus we speak of the **love** of God, **joy** of the Lord, and the **peace** of God.*
>
> *The **second cluster**–**patience**, **kindness** and **goodness** has to do with the kind of Christian we are, in our **outward** relationship to others. If we are unkind, and rude, short tempered, we lack the second cluster of fruit.*
>
> *The **third cluster** of spiritual fruit–**faith**, **meekness**, **temperance** (self-control) has to do with the **inward** man. Faith means to be faithful to our Christian commitments!"*

As we draw closer to God through Bible study, prayer, fasting, worship, and service, the desire to avoid sin will become a pleasure, and we gain a closer relationship with the Holy Spirit. Sinfulness will become repulsive, and one's willingness to do right and serve the Lord with practical love would not diminish because the old desires and unrestrained longings for sinful pleasures will fade. The soul that seeks to be obedient can avoid the type of trap that ensnared Lot's wife—looking back. We can only attain the spiritual maturity of not looking back at the courtesy of God's grace and His all-powerful Spirit through Jesus Christ, our Lord.

> *Then he answered and spake unto me, saying, This is the word of the LORD unto Zerubbabel, saying, **not by might, nor by power, but by my spirit, saith the LORD of hosts**. (Zechariah 4:6, KJV)*

> *I can do all things through Christ which strengthens me.* (Philippians 4:13, KJV)

Holiness is the soul's condition that leaves Earth and enters Heaven, and Jesus is the Way through Whom we enter. Our Savior opens the portal and guides us through the narrow passage that Heaven has opened up for each soul. Without a doubt, we become wiser and more valuable to God's Kingdom as we begin to accept that Christ alone is life, and outside of Him is only death. Living for the flesh only leads downward to God's punishment of the unrepentant.

Therefore, a prayer request to achieve, maintain, and support holiness is one of the best prayers one can render. Sin erects a barrier to purity and demotes humility. Pride declares that it knows more than God does, and its way is the right way. But the Bible says that God resists the proud and gives grace to the humble. God is angry with the wicked sinner every day until that erring soul turns back to Him.

> *God judgeth the righteous, and* **God is angry with the wicked every day** *[He does not want them to go to Hell]. If he turn not, He will whet his sword; He hath bent his bow, and made it ready.* (**Psalms** *7:11-12, KJV*)

> **The Lord is slow to anger and great in power**, *and will not at all acquit the wicked: the LORD hath his way in the whirlwind and in the storm, and the clouds are the dust of his feet.* (**Nahum** *1:3, KJV*)

> **He that is slow to anger is better than the mighty**, *and he that ruleth his spirit than he that taketh a city.* (**Proverbs** *16:32, KJV*)

THE ENEMY OF HOLINESS

Sin blocks God from interacting with His children. Our heavenly Father wants to provide a divine standard of care, but He can only do that if we allow Him. Permitting Him is not just a verbal statement. A clean lifestyle in a well-kept soul invites Him, not a loud, repetitive prayer or long fast. It is only holiness that would do it.

Of course, no one is ever holy enough for God, not even the angels. This doesn't diminish angels' holiness because they are wholly sanctified beings that are superior to humans and live in God's glory. This is less about angels and more about the condition of fallen man. The angels are already in Heaven, but earthlings need help to stay humble and not fall victim to the sin that caused Adam and Eve's expulsion from Eden.

> *Look, **God does not even trust the angels**. Even the heavens are not absolutely pure in his sight. (Job 15:15, NLT)*

> *Behold, **He putteth no trust in his saints; yea, the heavens are not clean in His sight**. (Job 15:15, KJV)*

CONSUMPTION AND BEHAVIOR

Finally, sanctification results from what we spiritually consume, of what we feed our soul using our eyes, ears, mouth, hands, and feet. The soul is the human processing unit (HPU); it becomes more efficient or wasteful, more capable or more powerless, depending on the quality of spiritual fuel it ingests. By free will and lifestyle choices, each person creates their own unique blend of spiritual gasoline, and God will hold us accountable for the formula we concoct.

Our hands and feet can aid and abet the soul in wrongdoing. How can those four natural extensions of our body and soul be held liable for crimes against the Holy Spirit, against God himself? The soul is presented with options in the form of thoughts from Heaven or Hell, but it decides whether to actuate them. If it does and the HPU decides to process forbidden raw material, our palms, fists, legs, and toes (and any other body part) will function as accomplices in the crime.

> And **if thy right eye offend thee, pluck it out, and cast it from thee**; for it is profitable for thee that one of thy members should perish, and not that thy whole body should be cast into Hell. And **if thy right hand offend thee, cut it off, and cast it from thee**; for it is profitable for thee that one of thy members should perish, and not that thy whole body should be cast into Hell. (Matthew 5:29-30, KJV)

In a nutshell, we are only as holy as that which we consume. God will help us, of course, but we must begin and maintain a healthy diet, using our free will to accept that divine opportunity. To support a lifestyle of holiness, we must gird up the loins of our minds, which means to be careful about what we allow to enter our soul. We must thoroughly inspect all input.

> Wherefore **gird up the loins of your mind [or soul]**, be sober, and hope to the end for the grace that is to be brought unto you at the revelation of Jesus Christ. (1 Peter 1:13, KJV)

> Finally, brethren, **whatsoever things are true**, whatsoever things are **honest**, whatsoever things are **just**, whatsoever things are **pure**, whatsoever things are **lovely**, whatsoever things are of **good**

report; *if there be **any virtue**, and if there be any praise, think on these things.* (Philippians 4:8, KJV)

Steven Covey, the author of *The 7 Habits of Highly Effective People*, advises us to "begin with the end in mind." In the context of holiness, let's "live with eternity in mind." That's where we are going, and sanctification through Jesus is the ticket back home. Have a safe journey.

VERSES ABOUT SANCTITY (HOLINESS)

1. For this is the will of God, your sanctification: that you should abstain from sexual immorality; that each of you should know how to possess his own vessel in sanctification and honor, not in passion of lust, like the Gentiles who do not know God. (1 Thessalonians 4:3-5, NKJV)
2. I beseech you therefore, brethren, by the mercies of God, that you present your bodies a living sacrifice, holy, acceptable to God, which is your reasonable service. (Romans 12:1, NKJV)
3. Do you not know that the unrighteous will not inherit the kingdom of God? Do not be deceived. Neither fornicators, nor idolaters, nor adulterers, nor homosexuals, nor sodomites, nor thieves, nor covetous, nor drunkards, nor revilers, nor extortioners will inherit the kingdom of God. (1 Corinthians 6:9-10, NKJV)

DO THIS TODAY AND MAKE IT A LIFESTYLE

1. Think right and do right.

2. Do not think anything of anyone you would not honestly render face to face.
3. Ask for forgiveness and pursue repentance to remain spiritually clean, healthy, and Heaven-ready.
4. Do not go to sleep with a heart pent up with hate or bitterness; tomorrow is not promised. The impure in heart will not see God.
5. Manage your life and time sensibly, like the wise virgins in Mathew 25.

SUMMARY POINTS

1. Holiness begins in eternity because it resides in the heart—the soul—and never leaves the spiritual world. Thoughts and deeds originate in the soul, and holiness—or the lack thereof—reflects the soul's condition. It is visible to God and angels in the spirit realm and is often accessible in plain sight to other mortals.
2. Without holiness or purity, no person will see God, and no one will get back home.
3. If a soul were a battery, a sanctified soul would be fully charged with sufficient energy to make it back home.
4. The offering of atonement for sin, using the blood of bulls and goats, was done by imperfect priests, and that process couldn't make anyone perfect. Perfection was accomplished by the one-time death of Christ on the cross, which allows us fallen beings to reenter Heaven.
5. Jesus is the divine offering, transforming the soul into perfection once and for all through salvation and sanctification.
6. Sanctification is the process of living an obedient life, day by day. It requires a willingness to get up every time we fall to remain on the narrow road.
7. The Earth is a place for spiritual adjustments and refinements; sanctification is the profitable management of this process.
8. Sanctification is our offering of service, self-denial, and spiritual sobriety.
9. Maintaining a lifetime of holiness requires a long-term, persistent, and patient investment strategy of

life and time so that one can yield a favorable return on Earth and in the hereafter.
10. We must remember that the same three attacks that caused Adam and Eve to fall are the ones we must overcome: the lust of the flesh, the lust of the eyes, and the pride of life.
11. Sanctification results from what we spiritually consume, of what we feed our soul using our eyes, ears, mouth, hands, and feet.
12. Jesus knows we will make mistakes along the way, but He never wants us to feel condemned. He did not come to condemn anyone. He knows we would need help every day.
13. Do not let your soul be forever lost due to mismanagement of free will. Operate profitably and continue to grow in sanctification as you die to self.

---

1. And Enoch walked with God: and he was not; for God took him. (Genesis 5:24, KJV)

III

7 PRAYERS FOR THE JOURNEY

PROGRESSING THROUGH PRAYER

1. Praise and thanksgiving to God - confession of sin.

2. Your family.

3. The President, your pastor, church, missionaries, etc.

4. The sick, bereaved, needy, and imprisoned.

5. Yourself - your personal spiritual growth, needs and wants.

You may use this illustration to manage your prayer time. (Image courtesy of Hope Aglow Ministries, Basic Doctrine Bible Study Course)

Rejoice evermore. ***Pray without ceasing.*** *(1 Thessalonians 5:16-17, KJV)*

*I **exhort therefore, that, first of all, supplications, prayers, intercessions, and giving of thanks, be made for all men;** for kings, and for all that are in authority; that we may lead a quiet and peaceable* life in all godliness and honesty. *(1 Timothy 2:1-2, KJV)*

Praying always with all prayer and supplication in the Spirit, and watching thereunto with all perseverance and supplication for all saints. *(Ephesians 6:18, KJV)*

And all things, **whatsoever ye shall ask in prayer, believing, ye shall receive.** *(Matthew 21:22, KJV)*

But the end of all things is at hand; **be ye therefore sober, and watch unto prayer.** *(1 Peter 4:7, KJV)*

Abstain from all appearance of evil. And the very God of peace sanctify you wholly; and I pray God your whole spirit and soul and body be preserved blameless unto the coming of our Lord Jesus Christ. Faithful is He that calleth you, who also will do it. *(1 Thessalonians 5:22-24, KJV)*

And take heed to yourselves, lest at any time your hearts be overcharged with surfeiting, and drunkenness, and cares of this life, and so that day come upon you unawares. For as a snare shall it come on all them that dwell on the face of the whole Earth. **Watch ye therefore, and <u>pray</u> always, that ye may be accounted worthy to escape all these things that shall come to pass**, and to stand before the Son of man. *(Luke 21:34-36, KJV)*

But the LORD shall endure for ever: He hath prepared his throne for judgment. And **He shall judge the** *world in righteousness, He shall minister judgment to the people in uprightness.* (Psalms 9:7-8, KJV)

PRAYER OF SALVATION
RESCUED BY JESUS

The following is a powerful prayer of commitment to Christ and one's eternal future. Read it first, then decidedly confess to God with heartfelt intention. Instead of writing another prayer of salvation, I believe the one provided by prophet Celestial of *The Master's Voice* prophecy blog is more than adequate.

> *If you confess with your mouth the Lord Jesus and believe in your heart God has raised Him from the dead, you will be saved. (Romans 10:9, NKJV)*
>
> **Death and life** *are in the power of the tongue. (Proverbs 18:21, KJV)*
>
> **Heavenly Father God,**
>
> I come to You in the bent and broken posture of true repentance.
> I have realized that on my own I am not able to

live any perfect life before You and I am sorry for that.

I have grieved Your Holy Spirit by my thoughts, words and actions Lord; I am not able to serve You as you require, not on my own.

I ask Your help today to be forgiven of all my sins, and given a new lifeline in the Person of Your Son Jesus Christ.

I have heard the words of Your mouth and I believe that there is no other worthy to be called GOD except You.

Now with my heart I believe that Jesus died for my sins and to purchase me from Hell, and I confess with my mouth that He is the only Lord of all.

Heavenly Father, please accept my repentance today.

Have mercy on me and favor me, and accept me into Your family.

Wash my sins away with the Blood of Jesus.

Cleanse me God, and baptize me with the fire of the Holy Spirit to remove every trace of my sinful past.

I want to belong to You, to walk with You, to know You as you already know me.

I turn away right now from my old life, and I renounce everything I used to do that was evil in Your eyes.

I ask for strength of the Holy Spirit to resist sin and temptation so that I don't return to my old life.

I choose Jesus Christ today as my Lord and Savior. Thank You God for hearing my prayer, I mean it from my heart and confess it with my mouth right now- JESUS CHRIST IS LORD.
In Jesus name I pray, amen. [1]

— PRAYER OF SALVATION, CELESTIAL

---

1. https://the-masters-voice.com/basics/

1

RECOGNIZE YOUR BLESSINGS
KNOW THAT GOD OWES US NOTHING

And the prayer of faith shall save the sick, and the Lord shall raise him up, and if he has committed sins, they shall be forgiven him. (James 5:15, KJV)

Confess your faults one to another, and pray one for another, that ye may be healed. **The effectual fervent prayer of a righteous man availeth much.** *(James 5:16, KJV)*

Dear Lord,

Jesus, thank You for everything You have done for us, and thank You for being God.

I praise and worship You, Mighty King.

I glorify and exalt You as the only One Who is worthy of honor and praise.

I worship You because of Who You are: Lord of Lords, King of kings, Holy one of Israel, and Master of everything. You are worthy of all praise.

Lord, I thank You for Your mercy, kindness, and compassion.

Thank You for another opportunity to pray, to call upon Your precious, all-powerful name—Your name of hope, strength, and value.

Thank You for another chance to get my life right and to obtain forgiveness.
Thank You for loving us and for all You do, seen and unseen.

Thank You for healing us by Your stripes, as Your Word says.

Thank You for allowing us to be clothed in our right, healthy minds, and please remember those who are not—please, by Your grace, mercy, and healing power, help them, I pray.

Thank You for where You have brought us from and for

where You are taking us, help us be led and managed by Your Holy Spirit, the Spirit of Truth.

Thank You for our families and for sustaining them.

Thank You for taking care of us all, day by day, night after night.

In Jesus' Name.
Thank you, my precious Lord.

2

SEEK DELIVERANCE
CUT TIES TO SINS

He has sent me to proclaim release to the captives and recovery of sight to the blind, to set free the oppressed. (Luke 4:18, CSB)

Dear Jesus,

Set us free in every area of our lives and help us to show our appreciation for what You are doing by pleasing You in thoughts and deeds, through holiness.

At this time, bless us, Your children, with wisdom, discernment, humility, and power to do Your will.

We come to You now asking for forgiveness of all our sins: sins of omission, and sins of commission, those we knowingly committed and those we are unaware of.

Lord, please help us to forgive those who have hurt us, as we would like You to forgive us for our many transgressions.

Thank You for Your love, forgiveness, and great faithfulness to us.

In Jesus' Name.
Thank You, Jesus, my Savior.

3

STRIVE FOR SOBERNESS

REALIZE THAT EVIL INTOXICATES

> Be sober-minded, be alert. Your adversary the devil is prowling around like a roaring lion, looking for anyone he can devour. (1 Peter 5:8, CSB)

Dear Lord,

Please help us to be sober enough to recognize our faults and to believe and realize that You alone can help and save us.

Teach us how to prophesy and proclaim life in all situations, discomfort and uncertainty.

Cause us to comprehend the power of words, which means life or death, because You have said there is life and death in the tongue.

Help us speak life, not death; success, not failure; love, not hate; Your truths, not the enemy's lies.

Please help us to read and study Your Word and to live it.

Jesus, help us live righteously in Your sight—wake us up, we beseech You so that we might be aware of Your presence and guidance.

Teach us and help us to understand the need and importance of holiness, without which no one will see You or be able to enter Heaven.

Please help us walk in the authority and power You have given to us through Jesus Christ and Your Holy Spirit.
In Jesus' Name.
Thank You, Lord.

4

REMAIN IN CHRIST

FOCUS ON HIM: HE IS ALIVE

Set your minds on things above, not on earthly things.
(Colossians 3:2, CSB)

Dear God,

I bind up every ruling spirit against us, every demonic spirit that seeks to enslave us and prevent us from coming to You and doing Your will.

I pray You would cripple the enemy and set us free.

In Jesus' name, I command every foul spirit to loosen

our souls and bodies. Heal and cleanse my heart, oh Lord.

Lord, where applicable, strengthen and protect every apostle, prophet, evangelist, pastor, teacher, and layperson, and grant them wisdom I pray.

I ask for the anointing (on our lives) that destroys every oppressive yoke, letting Your power flow freely through us.

I plead the blood of Jesus over us and command freedom, in Jesus' name, upon us.
I bind up, cast down, and crush the spirit of self-hatred in Jesus' name.

Lord, please help us to recognize and appreciate our value in You.
In Jesus' Name.
Thank You, my heavenly Father.

5

EXERCISE YOUR AUTHORITY
REIGN OVER EVIL

One day Jesus called together his twelve apostles and gave them authority over all demons—power to cast them out—and to heal all diseases. (Luke 9:1, TLB)

Dear conquering Savior, King Jesus,

I bind up every Jezebel spirit and those of stubbornness, rebellion, defiance, pride, and disobedience, in Jesus' name, I pray; I ask You to free us, oh Lord.
Go now, Jezebel, in Jesus' name, I command you.

In Jesus' name, I command our bodies and souls, our

hearts and minds, to line up according to the Word of God.

I bind up all spirits of confusion, division, frustration, and irritation; be gone now in Jesus' name, I pray.

I command all spirits of laziness, uncleanliness, mind control, and all spirits of distraction to loose us in Jesus' name.

I call for a clear mind, the mind of Christ, that we think as You think, that we desire as You desire.

Lord, help us retain divine knowledge and wisdom and remain focused on You, in Jesus' name, I pray.

In Jesus' name, I bind up the works of the enemy.

Jesus, please free us of every type of curse, disease, loneliness, suicide, failure, danger, and destruction —protect us from all evil, from all accidents.

I bind up spirits of **the lust of eyes, the lust of the flesh** and **pride of life**, in Jesus' name.

I take authority over all witchcraft, magic, hexes, and spells of hoodoo and voodoo.

I renounce all involvement with astrology, including occultic practices [1] and all demonic activity, in Jesus' name.

I renounce and neutralize all witches, warlocks,

wizards, grand wizards, high priests, and Satan himself in Jesus' name.

I come against all Satan's regional and territorial queens and witches in Jesus' name.

I bind up and deactivate every witch and demonic activity, and every plan formed against us, in Jesus' name.

I denounce all python spirits and every curse sent to us through the air, in Jesus' name.

With intense heat, I neutralize any curse spoken over us, in Jesus' name; I command every word meant for evil to fall to the ground and never rise again, for I bind up all their powers in the name of Jesus.

I bind up all drug and alcohol spirits, all hustling, worldly, and transferring spirits, including all street and greed spirits.

I shackle all spirits of fighting, lying and deception, hurt and misery, and I command them to free us in Jesus' name.

I bind up all spirits of illiteracy, deafness and dumbness, false burdens, cursed food, and any other cursed item; Lord, please reveal them to us and give us the will and strength to resist them, in Jesus' name.

I bind up all hindrances, worrying, tormenting fear,

doubt, and unbelief. I bind up all gossiping spirits and every spirit of bondage in Jesus' name.

I command them to leave us now in Jesus' name.

I cancel the contract and terminate the assignment of poverty, sickness, and death over God's people everywhere.

I break every band around our minds, yoke around our necks, wrists, and every shackle around our ankles and feet, in Jesus' name.

Lord, please blind the eyes of the dark side, deafen their ears, gag their mouths, bind their hands, shackle their feet, and confuse their minds in Jesus' name.

I plead, and in Your mighty name, Lord, cancel every spirit of retaliation, backlashing, and vengefulness (from the underworld) in Jesus' name, I pray.

In Jesus' Name.
Thank You, Jesus.

---

1. https://digitaloccultlibrary.commons.gc.cuny.edu/cults-and-the-occult/

6

PETITION FOR RESTORATION
LIVE IN HARMONY WITH EVERYONE

Blessed are the peacemakers, for they will be called sons of God. (Matthew 5:9, CSB)

Dear Father in Heaven,

In the name of our Lord and Savior, Jesus Christ, I ask for love, joy, peace, and the fruit of Your Spirit, Lord.

I ask that You fill us with the gifts of your Spirit to replace the spirits that have been cast out, in Jesus' name. Help us to resist inviting them again; strengthen us to live clean lives, in Jesus' name.

Help us to understand that we give the enemy power by our disobedience.

Help us to conduct lives that are consecrated to Your will, oh Lord.

Help us to hear and fear You, promptly respond to You, and live obediently before You.

Help us to desire You, to thirst after righteousness, and to shun even the appearance of evil.

Help us to stop procrastinating, and give us the understanding, discernment, and strength to do Your will.

Help us to hate evil and pursue good.

In Jesus' Name.
Thank you, sweet Lord.

7

GIVE THANKS
HE LIKES TO HEAR FROM YOU

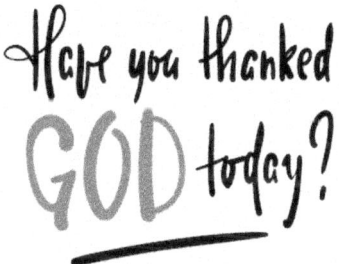

> *Rejoice evermore. **Pray without ceasing.** In every thing give thanks, for this is the will of God in Christ Jesus concerning you.* (1 Thessalonians 5:16-18, KJV)

God allows different seasons or situations in our lives, but He cannot change; He is always faithful and approachable. So let's give Him thanks for all He does.

Precious Jesus,

I thank You for hearing my prayer.

I thank You for power and authority over every evil spirit in Jesus' name.

I thank You for loving us. I thank You for making Your people the head and not the tail.

Thank You for working out every situation that concerns us for our good—strengthen us to have confidence in this truth, especially in hard times.

Please help us to quietly and patiently trust You without pride and anxiety.

By Your power, I thank You that nothing can pluck us from your hands, and I thank You that Your Word is truth.

I pray this prayer in the precious and matchless name of Jesus. AMEN, AMEN, and AMEN.

Special thanks to Quenitra Lewis Butler for providing the initial draft of these prayers.

PRAISE JESUS
MY ALL IN ALL

*J*have included the lyrics for "Crown Him with Many Crowns," as a special dedication to my ALL IN ALL: Jesus. The words are an expression of my thankfulness to He who has added immeasurable value to my life. I love you, Jesus. You may take a listen here: https://tinyurl.com/ym2vw3z9

1 Crown Him with many crowns,
the Lamb upon his throne.
Hark! how the heavenly anthem drowns
all music but its own.
Awake, my soul, and sing
of Him who died for thee,
and hail Him as thy matchless king
through all eternity.

2 Crown Him the Lord of life,
who triumphed o'er the grave,
and rose victorious in the strife
for those He came to save;
his glories now we sing

who died and rose on high,
who died eternal life to bring,
and lives that death may die.

3 Crown Him *the Lord of love;*
behold his hands and side,
rich wounds, yet visible above,
in beauty glorified;
no angels in the sky
can fully bear that sight,
but downward bends their burning eye
at mysteries so bright.

4 Crown Him *the Lord of years,*
the potentate of time,
creator of the rolling spheres,
ineffably sublime.
All hail, Redeemer, hail!
for thou hast died for me;
thy praise shall never, never fail
throughout eternity.

— CROWN HIM WITH MANY CROWNS,
MATTHEW BRIDGES (1851)

REFERENCES

CONSIDERABLE MENTIONS

2 Timothy 2:15, NKJV
"Study to shew thyself approved unto God, a workman that needeth not to be ashamed, rightly dividing the Word of truth."

Most of the following are not direct references in this guide. Nonetheless, I have included them because I have found them interesting enough to share with you.

- Melvin, B. W. (2018). *A land unknown: Hell's dominion.* Xulon Press.
- The University of Sydney. (2017, October 16). 4 Reasons Why Food Is More Important Than You Think. Retrieved from: https://tinyurl.com/yb6abxpy
- https://www.wogim.org/sinlist.htm
- Dove, Laurie. (2014, October 3). Do plants feel pain? *HowStuffWorks.com.* Retrieved from: https://tinyurl.com/y9xzp2mb
- Fraim, J. (2013, August 1). The Importance Of Symbols In Stories. Retrieved from: https://tinyurl.com/y4b5ylhl
- Strauss, Lehman. (2017, May). Man A Trinity (Spirit, Soul, Body). Retrieved from: https://goo.gl/WuZXPm
- John, Spacey. (2019, May 21). 47 Examples of the Human Experience. Simplicable. Retrieved from: https://tinyurl.com/y3cy6uws
- The Worst Part of Pompeii's Destruction Isn't What You Think — https://www.youtube.com/watch?v=rduUDoy3dYE

- Schrodinger, Erwin. What is Life? (Canto Classics) (p. 2). Cambridge University Press. Kindle Edition.
- Clifton, Jim. (2017, June 13). The World's Broken Workplace. Retrieved from: https://tinyurl.com/y3alsfry
- Nally, J. R. (2017, August 14). 1. An Eternal Hell Is for Real - 1. The Heresy of Annihilationism? Retrieved February 05, 2021, from https://tinyurl.com/3kd3lcl5
- Nosweatshakespeare.com. (2020, October 06). The seven ages of man. Retrieved February 06, 2021, from https://tinyurl.com/y7nk3w3z
- The history of barcodes. (2016, August 30). Retrieved February 11, 2021, from https://tinyurl.com/49rkxpb9
- Britannica, T. Editors of Encyclopaedia (2018, April 26). *Mina. Encyclopedia Britannica.* https://www.britannica.com/science/mina-unit-of-weight

WATCH ME FIRST

The Lord is warning the church. Retrieved from https://tinyurl.com/5x3whvax

TIMELY VIDEOS ABOUT HELL AND HEAVEN

1. The Hour of Revelation by Deaconess Jane Mensah [Rapture]. Retrieved from https://tinyurl.com/y5p9tve7
2. Better Get Saved Today. Retrieved from https://goo.gl/C3EeHD
3. I Sing Praises to Your Name (Worship song). Retrieved from https://youtu.be/i6hoDCrlOOA

4. I Saw Old Lady In Hell! Retrieved from https://youtu.be/wh4oYfy6Il4
5. Don't expect a breakthrough if you do not obey. Retrieved from https://tinyurl.com/y6am3vqe
6. Escape From Hell Ex Radical Muslim Testimony. Retrieved from https://youtu.be/8aGAD3tBUQ8
7. Ex Satan Worshipper John Ramirez Testimony. Retrieved from https://goo.gl/BqhgeW
8. Experience of Heaven and Hell! She saw Pop Stars who were Tortured in Hell. Retrieved from https://tinyurl.com/y5undxoh
9. Heaven and Hell Experiences (NDEs) Dr. Rawlings MD. Retrieved from https://goo.gl/TZPSkt
10. Heaven is so Real by Choo Thomas. Retrieved from
11. https://tinyurl.com/y4lywlwy)
12. How to Refuse the RFID Chip Like a BOSS.. Retrieved from https://goo.gl/4aZpNF
13. Mary K Baxter Describes Horrors of Hell. Retrieved from https://tinyurl.com/znvvvcp
14. Rapture & Great Tribulation. Retrieved from https://goo.gl/HDJJpu
15. RFID, Technology and THE MARK. Retrieved from https://goo.gl/sndAPh
16. Shawn Weed's Hell Testimony. Retrieved from https://tinyurl.com/yy8zlwq6
17. URGENT: 23 Minutes in Hell. Retrieved from https://goo.gl/7mPS3x
18. URGENT: A Visit at the Gates of Hell. Retrieved from https://youtu.be/jeEv08UdRxg
19. URGENT: I saw Heaven. Retrieved from https://youtu.be/_X5dc_Zd5mo
20. 66 Charles Capps Understanding Faith 01 of 3. Retrieved from https://tinyurl.com/y6525nep
21. Vital Facts You Must Know About The Mark of The

Beast (RFID Chip). Retrieved from https://goo.gl/YJ6cEQ
22. What Is Christian Persecution? .Retrieved from https://goo.gl/FrVFCE

THE RAPTURE

1. 69 Charles Capps - The Rapture . Retrieved from https://goo.gl/8mMhfF
2. 70 Charles Capps Endtimes 01 of 4 . Retrieved from https://goo.gl/qoEU32
3. 71 Charles Capps - Endtimes 02 of 4 . Retrieved from https://goo.gl/YgExrq
4. 75 Charles Capps - The Coming of the Lord . Retrieved from https://goo.gl/xkvh41
5. 76 Charles Capps - Endtimes EMIC) 1999 . Retrieved from https://goo.gl/BXXquR
6. Are You Ready For the Coming of Jesus by David Wilkerson . Retrieved from https://tinyurl.com/y4d2y29h
7. The 2nd Coming of Jesus - New World Order by David Wilkerson .Retrieved from https://tinyurl.com/y4wd2pbp

ABOUT THE AUTHOR

Wyne Ince doesn't consider himself a theologian, preacher, or even formally trained in delivering God's instructions. His book, *Thoughts of Life and Time: Strategies for Living a Complete Life*, is an inspirational guide that takes the reader through the journey of understanding these mission-critical operations: (1) why God sent us to Earth, (2) how we should spend His investment of life and time in us, and (3) how we can plan to return to Heaven.

He received his bachelor's degree in Computer Information Systems from the City University of New York (CUNY). He then pursued his master's in telecommunication and information management from the Polytechnic Institute of New York University (NYU). He has been a follower of Jesus Christ for many years. To remain persistent and focused on the narrow road, he regularly practiced praising, praying, fasting, and what is pleasing in the eyes of God.

NOTES

NOTES

NOTES

www.ingramcontent.com/pod-product-compliance
Lightning Source LLC
Chambersburg PA
CBHW071650090426
42738CB00009B/1483